Treating PTSD With Cognitive-Behavioral Therapies

Concise Guides
on Trauma Care Book Series

Treating PTSD With Cognitive-Behavioral Therapies:
Interventions That Work
Candice M. Monson and Philippe Shnaider

Treating PTSD With Cognitive-Behavioral Therapies

Interventions That Work

Candice M. Monson and Philippe Shnaider

American Psychological Association • Washington, DC

Published by
American Psychological Association
750 First Street, NE
Washington, DC 20002
www.apa.org

To order
APA Order Department
P.O. Box 92984
Washington, DC 20090-2984
Tel: (800) 374-2721; Direct: (202) 336-5510
Fax: (202) 336-5502; TDD/TTY: (202) 336-6123
Online: www.apa.org/pubs/books
E-mail: order@apa.org

In the U.K., Europe, Africa, and the Middle East, copies may be ordered from
American Psychological Association
3 Henrietta Street
Covent Garden, London
WC2E 8LU England

Typeset in Minion by Circle Graphics, Inc., Columbia, MD

Printer: United Book Press, Baltimore, MD
Cover Designer: Mercury Publishing Services, Inc., Rockville, MD
Cover Art: Betsy Bauer, *Vista Luminosa VI*, 2011, Oil on Panel, 6″ × 6″

The opinions and statements published are the responsibility of the authors, and such opinions and statements do not necessarily represent the policies of the American Psychological Association.

Library of Congress Cataloging-in-Publication Data
Monson, Candice M.
  Treating PTSD with cognitive-behavioral therapies : interventions that work / by Candice M. Monson and Philippe Shnaider. — First edition.
      pages cm
  Includes bibliographical references and index.
  ISBN-13: 978-1-4338-1737-3
  ISBN-10: 1-4338-1737-3
1. Post-traumatic stress disorder—Treatment. 2. Cognitive therapy. I. Shnaider, Philippe. II. Title. III. Title: Treating post traumatic stress disorder with cognitive-behavioral therapies.
  RC552.P67M67 2014
  616.85'21—dc23
                                        2013044027

British Library Cataloguing-in-Publication Data
A CIP record is available from the British Library.

Printed in the United States of America
First Edition

http://dx.doi.org/10.1037/14372-000

Contents

Series Foreword

Exposure to traumatic events is all too common, in turn increasing the risk for a range of significant mental problems, such as posttraumatic stress disorder (PTSD) and depression; physical health problems; negative health behaviors, such as smoking and excessive alcohol consumption; poor social and occupational functioning; and overall low quality of life. As mass traumas (e.g., September 11th, military engagements in Iraq and Afghanistan, disasters such as Hurricane Katrina) have propelled trauma into a brighter public spotlight, the numbers of trauma survivors seeking services for mental health consequences will likely continue to increase. Despite the far-ranging consequences of trauma and the high rates of exposure, relatively little emphasis is placed on trauma education in undergraduate and graduate psychology programs in the United States. Calls for action have appeared in the American Psychological Association's journal *Psychological Trauma: Theory, Research, Practice, and Policy* with such articles as "The Need for Inclusion of Psychological Trauma in the Professional Curriculum: A Call to Action" by Christine A. Courtois and Steven N. Gold and "The Art and Science of Trauma-Focused Training and Education" by Anne DePrince and Elana Newman. The lack of education in the assessment and treatment of trauma and related clinical issues at undergraduate and graduate levels increases the urgency of our need to develop effective trauma resources for students as well as postgraduate professionals.

This book series, Concise Guides on Trauma Care, addresses that urgent need by providing truly translational books that bring the best of trauma psychology science to mental health professionals working in diverse settings. To do so, the series will focus on what we know (and do not know) about specific trauma topics, with attention to how trauma psychology science translates to diverse populations (diversity broadly defined, in terms of development, ethnicity, socioeconomic status, sexual orientation, and so forth).

This series represents one of many efforts undertaken by Division 56 (Trauma Psychology) of the American Psychological Association to advance trauma training and education (e.g., see http://www.apatraumadivision. org/resources.php). We are pleased to work with Division 56 and a volunteer editorial board to develop this series, which is officially launched with the publication of this important book on cognitive-behavioral interventions for adults diagnosed with PTSD. Monson and Shnaider's inaugural book provides an engaging, thoughtful, and concise overview of research and practical considerations in the use of cognitive-behavioral treatment strategies with adult clients. Future books in the series will build on the foundation set by this book to address a range of assessment, treatment, and developmental issues in trauma care.

Anne DePrince
Ann T. Chu
Series Editors

Treating PTSD With Cognitive-Behavioral Therapies

Introduction

Over the past 30 years, there has been an explosion in the development and testing of cognitive-behavioral therapies (CBTs) for posttraumatic stress disorder (PTSD). Clinical research has consistently demonstrated that these therapies are among the most efficacious treatments for PTSD (for reviews, see Bisson & Andrew, 2009; Bisson et al., 2007; Bradley, Greene, Russ, Dutra, & Westen, 2005; Resick, Monson, & Gutner, 2007) and that trauma-focused CBTs are recommended as first-line treatments for the disorder (American Psychiatric Association, 2004; Australian Centre for Posttraumatic Mental Health, 2007; Foa, Keane, Friedman, & Cohen, 2009; Management of Post-Traumatic Stress Working Group, 2010; National Institute for Health and Care Excellence, 2005).

This book aims to guide clinicians through existing CBT interventions for adults with PTSD by briefly presenting the theoretical underpinnings of empirically supported interventions, providing an overview

http://dx.doi.org/10.1037/14372-001
Treating PTSD With Cognitive-Behavioral Therapies: Interventions That Work, by C. M. Monson and P. Shnaider

of the treatment elements themselves, and reviewing treatment packages that have been put forth comprising these interventions (e.g., prolonged exposure, cognitive processing therapy, stress-inoculation training). We distinguish between therapies that are predominantly behavioral and cognitive, and between those that are trauma-focused versus non–trauma-focused. We discuss common problems and provide ways to troubleshoot them when necessary, and we conclude with a discussion of promising practices in, and future directions for, CBT for PTSD. Finally, we provide suggested readings for clinicians wishing to further develop their clinical skills in treating PTSD.

The book is written to be as clinician friendly as possible to increase the likelihood that clinicians will use these interventions with their clients. Although learning and providing these interventions may be more up-front work for clinicians who are not familiar with their delivery, we have observed that clinicians who have endeavored to learn and apply these interventions improve their clinical practice skills more generally. To illustrate the concepts, we have included a number of case examples that have been adequately disguised to protect client confidentiality. Ultimately, we hope that this book results in more clients with PTSD receiving evidence-based therapies that hold good promise to improve their symptoms and well-being.

Several meta-analyses and reviews have now established the efficacy of CBT for adults with PTSD (e.g., Bisson & Andrew, 2009; Bisson et al., 2007; Bradley et al., 2005). Although CBT is a class of treatments, there are specific cognitive and behavioral interventions that have been established to work in treating PTSD and its common comorbidities. These interventions and treatment packages can be divided into those that are trauma-focused and those that are non–trauma-focused.

The term *trauma-focused CBT* means that the specific interventions used to treat PTSD are aimed at memories, reminders, and/or distorted beliefs related to the traumatic event. In these therapies, details of the traumatic event are disclosed, memories and reminders are approached, and maladaptive or distorted beliefs about why the traumatic event occurred and what it means in the here-and-now are discussed. Although all trauma-focused CBT interventions require some level of disclosure about the traumatic event, the degree to which details are revealed and discussed depends on the specific treatment strategies or package used.

In contrast, the term *non–trauma-focused CBT* describes interventions aimed at addressing problematic behaviors and cognitions in the here-and-now without referring back to or recounting the traumatic event. This present-centered approach provides clients with cognitive-behavioral strategies to manage the PTSD symptoms that are currently interfering or causing distress in their lives, and it addresses problems that are often associated with, or result from, PTSD (e.g., depression, social isolation). Interventions used to improve stress and anxiety management, such as relaxation training, breathing retraining, and positive self-talk, are often employed in non–trauma-focused CBT.

Treatment outcome studies primarily support the use of trauma-focused CBT for PTSD over non–trauma-focused approaches (for reviews, see Bisson & Andrew, 2009; Bisson et al., 2007; Bradley et al., 2005; Ehlers et al., 2010). However, there is evidence for the efficacy of non–trauma-focused interventions in improving PTSD, and this class of interventions may be particularly relevant for clients who are unwilling to endeavor trauma-focused interventions. Among the trauma-focused CBT interventions, exposure to trauma-related memories and reminders, a behavioral technique, has received the most empirical investigation to date. Several studies have documented the efficacy of both imaginal and in vivo exposure techniques (e.g., Bryant, Moulds, Guthrie, Dang, & Nixon, 2003; Richards, Lovell, & Marks, 1994; Tarrier, Pilgrim, et al., 1999). Furthermore, an exposure-based treatment package (i.e., prolonged exposure) has received substantial support (for a review, see Powers, Halpern, Ferenschak, Gillihan, & Foa, 2010). Similarly, trauma-focused cognitive interventions have been shown to efficaciously treat PTSD, with evidence supporting this technique in isolation as well as in treatment packages that are primarily cognitive in nature (i.e., cognitive processing therapy, cognitive-behavioral therapy; Bryant et al., 2008; Chard, 2005; Ehlers, Clark, Hackmann, McManus, & Fennell, 2005; Forbes et al., 2012; Monson et al., 2006; Resick, Galovski, et al., 2008; Resick, Nishith, Weaver, Astin, & Feuer, 2002; Surís, Link-Malcolm, Chard, Ahn, & North, 2013).

Although to a lesser extent, non–trauma-focused CBT interventions and treatment packages have received support in the treatment of PTSD, they would profit from further investigation (Foa et al., 1999; Foa, Rothbaum, Riggs, & Murdock, 1991; Marks, Lovell, Noshirvani, Livanou, & Thrasher, 1998; Taylor et al., 2003; Vaughan et al., 1994). The non–trauma-focused CBT treatment package for PTSD with the best empirical support is stress-inoculation training (Meichenbaum, 1985), which provides trauma survivors a variety of cognitive and behavioral strategies to address stress and anxiety that have generalized after a traumatic event.

Empirical investigation of CBT interventions for PTSD has brought with it a number of findings relevant to clinical practice, such as the inclusion of clients with a myriad of comorbidities, demographic characteristics, and multiple traumatization, including clients whom others might label *complex trauma* patients. It is our experience that clients with single-incident traumas, no comorbidities, and few psychosocial impairments are those who are likely to recover naturally from their traumatization and do not necessarily need intervention. Short of acute issues related to client or other safety (i.e., imminent suicidality or homicidality, life-threatening self-harm, ongoing domestic violence) or stabilization of major psychopathology (e.g., mania, acute psychosis), the existing evidence gleaned from randomized controlled trials of PTSD treatment indicates that both trauma-focused and non–trauma-focused interventions are safe to deliver to those with PTSD. In fact, we argue that failure to provide these interventions outside of these circumstances is depriving trauma survivors of treatments that will shorten their period of suffering from PTSD, its comorbidities, and the psychosocial impairments that accompany these conditions. Clinicians may be inclined to provide supportive therapy to "stabilize" clients before initiating these therapies, which inadvertently prolongs the time to efficacious treatment and may teach coping skills (e.g., distraction, avoidance) that are actually antithetical to the interventions that have been shown to work with PTSD and its comorbities. Moreover, CBT interventions have been shown to improve the impairments that have been defined as complex trauma presentations, such as dissociation, sexual impairments, emotion dysregulation, identity disturbance, and cognitive distortions (e.g., Chard, 2005; Resick, Nishith, & Griffin, 2003).

PTSD treatment researchers have not generally elected to recruit pristine, single-problem samples of patients. In treatment trials, CBT successfully improves PTSD symptoms that have resulted from different types of traumas (e.g., combat, sexual and physical assault, natural disaster, motor vehicle accident), and its treatment effects are generally consistent, irrespective of time since traumatization, age, marital status, education, and employment (for reviews, see Bisson & Andrew, 2009; Management of Post-Traumatic Stress Working Group, 2010; Powers et al., 2010). Although some evidence suggests that women with PTSD may have a better response to treatment (Tarrier, Sommerfield, Pilgrim, & Faragher, 2000), others have not found significant sex differences in treatment response (Jaycox, Foa, & Morral, 1998; Marks et al., 1998). Furthermore, the use of CBT with cultural minorities and in individuals with low socioeconomic status has also resulted in successful treatment outcomes (e.g., Feske, 2008; Rosenheck & Fontana, 1996).

A second important and clinically relevant finding from treatment trials examining CBT is that treatment gains are maintained after these interventions. Many studies show successful maintenance of treatment outcomes at 3- to 6-month follow-up assessments, and some have demonstrated the preservation of these effects for up to a year after treatment (for reviews, see Bisson & Andrew, 2009; Management of Post-Traumatic Stress Working Group, 2010; Powers et al., 2010). Furthermore, a recent study found that patients treated with cognitive processing therapy and prolonged exposure maintained treatment gains at 5 or more years posttreatment (Resick, Williams, Suvak, Monson, & Gradus, 2012). These findings demonstrate the short- and long-term efficacy of CBT for PTSD across numerous individual and group differences, lending support for the utility of this treatment approach across various patients seen in clinical practice.

In efforts to increase the impact and expand the reach of CBT for PTSD, as well as to benefit from technological advances, researchers have examined different approaches to service delivery. At the current time, reviews and treatment guidelines do not recommend group CBT as a first-line treatment for PTSD, which is largely due to the lack of strong methodological research studies examining its efficacy. The extant research has found promising outcomes, and some treatment guidelines have recommended group CBT as an adjunctive treatment (e.g., American Psychiatric Association, 2004; Australian Centre for Posttraumatic Mental Health, 2007; Bisson & Andrew, 2009; Foa et al., 2009; Management of Post-Traumatic Stress Working Group, 2010; National Institute for Health and Care Excellence, 2005). Furthermore, studies utilizing trauma-focused group CBT in combination with individual treatment have shown positive outcomes, indicating that this may be an effective format for treatment delivery requiring additional investigation (e.g., Chard, 2005). Although limited in number, studies documenting the use of telehealth, videoconferencing, and Internet delivery options have also shown positive outcomes (for reviews, see Cukor, Spitalnick, Difede, Rizzo, & Rothbaum, 2009; Germain, Marchand, Bouchard, Drouin, & Guay, 2009; Hirai & Clum, 2005; Knaevelsrud & Maercker, 2007; Lange, van de Ven, & Schrieken, 2003; Litz, Engel, Bryant, & Papa, 2007; Tuerk, Yoder, Ruggiero, Gros, & Acierno, 2010). Although still in its infancy, research examining the efficacy of CBT using various service delivery options has shown promising outcomes. With continued examination of this domain of research, the years to come will better inform any modifications needed to existing treatments or factors to consider in order to maximize the benefit of these novel approaches to service delivery.

Another important conclusion based on a review of the CBT for PTSD treatment outcome literature to date is that there is minimal evidence indicating the superiority of one CBT intervention or package over another. Although there is some evidence that cognitive interventions may be superior for guilt-related cognitions and improving self-reported health problems (Galovski, Monson, Bruce, & Resick, 2009; Resick et al., 2002) and that high levels of anger may be an impediment to exposure therapy techniques (Foa, Riggs, Massie, & Yarczower, 1995), there are minimal data indicating that one should favor cognitive or behavioral therapy interventions for PTSD. In the absence of solid data for client–treatment matching, we believe that a more important factor is a given client's preference for receiving the different types of treatment interventions. Research has consistently documented that clients' understanding and belief in a given therapy rationale predict treatment outcomes (e.g., Abramowitz, Franklin, Zoellner, & Dibernardo, 2002; Addis & Jacobson, 2000). This notion is also consistent with the movement toward consumer-driven treatment decision-making in which clinicians review the various treatment options, as well as their related costs and benefits, and clients are actively involved in choosing their treatment (O'Connor et al., 2009). Given the current state of research on predictors of treatment response, we believe that client preference for the various types of interventions, based on a good description of the therapies and informed consent by the therapist with the client, should determine treatment planning. In the ideal circumstance, therapists will be prepared to deliver the range of evidence-based interventions for their clients with PTSD on the basis of client preference.

In spite of the overwhelming evidence supporting the efficacy of trauma-focused CBT for PTSD, studies have consistently found that clinicians underutilize these interventions, specifically exposure-based interventions (e.g., Becker, Zayfert, & Anderson, 2004; Rosen et al., 2004). There are a number of documented reasons for this gap between science and practice, including clinicians' fears that trauma-focused techniques will result in symptom exacerbation, assumptions that manualized treatments are too rigid for complex clients believed not to be included in treatment trials, and concerns that treatment outcome findings do not generalize to clinical practice settings outside of research settings (Becker et al., 2004; Feeny, Hembree, & Zoellner, 2003; Rosen et al., 2004). Many of these myths have been addressed (Feeny et al., 2003; van Minnen, Harned, Zoellner, & Mills, 2012); however, there is yet to be a shift in the use of empirically supported CBT. Myths about CBT for PTSD have the potential to be a barrier to the use of these techniques. Thus, in Table 1 we provide an overview of facts and myths about CBT for PTSD, in an effort to increase clinicians' desire to learn more about these techniques and enhance their confidence in using them.

Table 1

Facts and Myths About the Utilization of Cognitive-Behavioral Therapy (CBT) for Posttraumatic Stress Disorder (PTSD)

Facts	Myths
Trauma-focused CBT is indicated as a first-line treatment approach by numerous treatment guidelines.	Trauma-focused CBT will lead clients to get worse.
Clients with PTSD are likely to benefit most from trauma-focused CBT.	Clients will not be able to handle trauma-focused work such as exposure interventions.
Trauma-focused CBT has resulted in the maintenance of treatment gains for 5+ years posttreatment.	Complex clients will not improve.
	CBT for PTSD will not work for the populations seen in regular practice.
Trauma-focused CBT has been shown to be effective across different types of traumas.	Certain trauma-focused CBT interventions are more efficacious than others.
Clients with comorbidities often evidence improvements in the symptoms of other disorders following trauma-focused CBT.	It is not safe to do trauma-focused CBT with clients who have comorbidities.
	Engaging in trauma-focused treatment will increase the risk of suicide or self-injury.
	Clients need to do work to prepare themselves to address their traumas.
	Clients need a long time of working with their therapist before they can address their traumas.
	Clients will be retraumatized by doing trauma-focused CBT.
	Time will heal PTSD symptoms; trauma-focused therapy is unnecessary.
	Trauma-focused CBT works only for high-functioning clients.
	Focusing on the trauma will lead to increased dropout from therapy.
	Clients will not do trauma-focused CBT.
	Time-limited, structured trauma-focused therapy cannot fully address PTSD; it takes a long time to recover.

1

Theory Underlying Trauma-Focused Interventions

Understanding the theoretical models on which trauma-focused cognitive-behavioral therapy (CBT) is based is critical to individual case conceptualization and successful implementation of specific interventions for posttraumatic stress disorder (PTSD). The deeper one's understanding of the cognitive and behavioral factors that are postulated to lead to the onset and maintenance of PTSD, the better able one will be to think broadly and flexibly about how to implement treatment interventions and use trauma-focused treatment protocols with fidelity. In this chapter, we describe the prominent behavioral and cognitive theories that support the use of the related interventions, and we use a case example to facilitate conceptualization within each theory.

Consistent across the theories described below, PTSD is considered to be a disorder resulting from nonrecovery after traumatization. In other words, symptoms are not considered to *develop* over time like many other

http://dx.doi.org/10.1037/14372-002
Treating PTSD With Cognitive-Behavioral Therapies: Interventions That Work, by C. M. Monson and P. Shnaider

mental health conditions that have early warning signs or a prodromal phase (e.g., depression, schizophrenia). Rather, prospective studies indicate that in the acute aftermath of exposure to a traumatic event, most individuals will have an assortment of symptoms that if they do not abate, will later be defined as a PTSD. With time, most people will experience a decrease in their symptomatology and thereby *recover* naturally without intervention (Ehlers, Mayou, & Bryant, 1998; Riggs, Rothbaum, & Foa, 1995; Rothbaum, Foa, Riggs, Murdock, & Walsh, 1992). Evidence suggests that *delayed onset* cases (i.e., appearance of symptoms months or years after trauma exposure) of PTSD are most generally characterized by subthreshold diagnoses at prior evaluations (Bryant & Harvey, 2002; Buckley, Blanchard, & Hickling, 1996; Ehlers et al., 1998).

THEORY UNDERLYING BEHAVIORAL TRAUMA-FOCUSED INTERVENTIONS

Behavioral theorists explaining PTSD turned to Mowrer's (1960) early work on the development and maintenance of fear reactions more generally. The first part of Mowrer's two-part theory of fear responding is that classical conditioning processes explain the onset of PTSD symptoms via the pairing of an aversive environment (i.e., the trauma and associated stimuli) with a fear response. This salient instance, during which these stimuli are paired with fear, results in trauma memories and associated cues that can later evoke a fear response. Mowrer's theory goes on to explain that PTSD is maintained via operant conditioning principles, whereby avoidance of these stimuli is negatively reinforced through the fear reduction that follows from eliminating or escaping from these trauma cues and reminders.

Since that time, there have been efforts to expand on this theory to incorporate cognitive elements. In this vein, *emotional processing theory* (Foa & Kozak, 1986) is the most elaborated and researched theory supporting behavioral trauma-focused interventions for PTSD. Foa and Kozak (1986) built on Lang's (1977, 1979) concept of a fear structure, which is postulated to contain stimulus, response, and meaning elements that result in a fear response when activated. Although these structures can be adaptive, maladaptive or pathological fear structures can also develop. Later revised (Foa & McNally, 1996) and then applied specifically to PTSD (Foa, Huppert, & Cahill, 2006), emotional processing theory (Foa & Kozak, 1986) holds that individuals who have experienced traumatic events can develop problematic associations between trauma-related reminders, which are objectively safe in the present day (e.g., people, places, situations, memories), meaning elements (e.g., the world is dangerous, I am incompetent), and responses (e.g., avoidance of trauma reminders, emotional numbing), due to their experience with a salient and often life-threatening event. When these maladaptive associations and fear structures form, this theory holds that emotional processing (i.e., correcting the maladaptive fear structure) is the method by which to modify them.

As Foa et al. (2006) described in their application of this theory to PTSD, emotional processing is the method by which the fear structure is modified. For emotional processing to succeed, the existing fear structure must first be activated and, second, information incompatible with the fear structure must be presented (Foa & Kozak, 1986). With activation of the fear structure, the associations among its stimulus, response, and meaning elements are evoked.

The second element necessary to changing the fear structure is the presentation of information incompatible with it. This means that an individual's predicted outcome in a given situation needs to be disconfirmed. According to Foa and colleagues (Foa et al., 2006; Foa & Kozak, 1986; Foa & McNally, 1996), the process of receiving disconfirming information can occur through the nonoccurrence of the feared outcome and through the process of habituation. In the former case, individuals are able to reevaluate the likelihood of their predicted outcome occurring, thus modifying the fear structure. Habituation provides another method by which disconfirming information can be acquired by the client in order to modify the fear structure. *Habituation* refers to the diminishment of a physiological or emotional response that tends to occur via extended and repeated presentation of evocative stimuli. Foa and Kozak (1986) explained that habituation helps correct the predicted harm or costs associated with trauma-related cues. Through habituation, clients learn that the fear response will not last forever and that they can remain in control of their self and their emotions. Notably, although both within-session (i.e., decline of physiological and emotional response during a session) and between-session (i.e., decline of physiological and emotional response across treatment sessions) habituation may be beneficial and indicative of emotional processing (Foa & Kozak, 1986), between-session habituation has been more closely associated with symptom reduction (for a review, see Foa et al., 2006).

Emotional processing can occur in treatment with the systematic presentation of trauma-relevant stimuli. However, it is also used to explain why the majority of individuals who are exposed to a traumatic event will recover naturally from their posttraumatic responses and not be diagnosed with PTSD. In the case of natural recovery, individuals allow for contact with reminders of the traumatic event that activate the fear structure and provide disconfirming information to that originally held in the fear structure.

Emotional processing theory accounts for both natural recovery and recovery with clinical intervention. In the context of the former, individuals are said to naturally modify their maladaptive fear structures through interactions with, and confrontation of, trauma reminders, disclosure of the traumatic event, and thinking about the trauma without clinical intervention. In the context of treatment, individuals are systematically exposed to both the trauma memory through imaginal exposures (i.e., repeated retelling of trauma narrative) and trauma reminders in their day-to-day life through in vivo exposures (i.e., systematic exposure to trauma-related stimuli in current environment) in order to activate and modify the fear structure.

THEORY UNDERLYING COGNITIVE TRAUMA-FOCUSED INTERVENTIONS

Several cognitive theories have emerged supporting the use of trauma-focused cognitive interventions for PTSD (Beck, Emery, & Greenberg, 2005; Ehlers & Clark, 2000; Janoff-Bulman, 1989, 2010; Resick, Monson, & Chard, 2008). Given the current book's focus on putting research into practice and presenting information in a clinician-friendly and practical manner, we focus on one of the most prominent cognitive theories of PTSD, *social cognitive theory of PTSD,* because it underlies the cognitive treatment package called *cognitive processing theory* (Resick, Monson, & Chard, 2008), described in Chapter 3.

Social cognitive theory of PTSD holds that avoidance of thinking about the traumatic event, as well as problematic appraisals of a traumatic event when memories are faced, contributes to nonrecovery. More specifically, individuals who do not recover are believed to try to *assimilate* the traumatic event into previously held positive or negative beliefs about the self, others, and the world. Assimilation is the attempt individuals with PTSD make to construe the traumatic event in a way that makes it fit with their preexisting beliefs. A common example of assimilation in those with PTSD is *just-world thinking,* or the belief that good things happen to good people and bad things happen to bad people (Lerner, 1980). In the case of traumatic events (i.e., bad things), the individual assumes that she or he did something bad that may have led to the event, or that the event is punishment for something she or he may have done in the past. Another common type of assimilation is *hindsight bias,* or evaluating the event based on information that is only known after the fact (Fischhoff, 1975). For example, one of us had a client who served as a combatant in Iraq. He held the belief that he should not have joined the military and served in Iraq, because no weapons of mass destruction were found upon investigation. In this case, it was important to explore what the client knew at the time he joined the military after the 9/11 attacks, and not what he knew many years after his service.

Another common form of assimilation is *happily ever after thinking* (Monson & Fredman, 2012), or thinking that an alternative action would have led to a positive outcome. An example of this comes from our work with sexual assault victims, who often believe that if they would have fought back, they could have prevented their assault from happening, neglecting other possible untoward outcomes, including death or more serious injury. In essence, assimilation can be conceptualized as efforts to exert predictability and control over the traumatic event that paradoxically leave the traumatized individual with unprocessed traumatic material and related PTSD symptoms.

In social cognitive theory, problematic appraisals about traumatic events lead to, or seemingly confirm, overgeneralized maladaptive beliefs about the self, others, and the world after traumatization. In other words, individuals *overaccommodate* their beliefs on the basis of the traumatic experience. Overaccommodation is the attempt individuals with PTSD make to change their beliefs so that the trauma, and any negative sequelae, can be integrated into their beliefs. An example of overaccommodation is when an individual with PTSD considers the traumatic experience to be proof of preexisting negative beliefs. Borrowing from earlier work by McCann and Pearlman (1990), the theory identifies beliefs related to the self and others that are often overaccommodated and contribute to nonrecovery. These beliefs tend to be related to safety, trust, power/control, esteem, and intimacy. Social cognitive theory of PTSD allows for the idea that clients will have different preexisting beliefs in each area that may have been positive or negative based on their prior learning history. For example, prior positive beliefs in these areas may be challenged after a traumatic event (e.g., "I thought I could trust my judgment and the person who assaulted me") or prior negative beliefs could be seemingly confirmed (e.g., "I knew men could not be trusted").

The key to recovery, according to this theory, is to experience the *natural* emotions that the person with PTSD is avoiding or suppressing related to the traumatic event and to correct misappraisals about the trauma as well as current-day cognitions that have been disrupted and are causing *manufactured* emotions. Natural emotions are described as the hardwired emotions that emanate directly from the traumatic experience. For example, during a traumatic event it is natural to feel fear that one might be injured or killed, or to feel disgust and horror at witnessing something atrocious. In this model, natural emotions, if approached and experienced, have a self-limiting course and energy. They do not perpetuate themselves, and thereby, contrary to behavioral theories of PTSD, do not require interventions aimed at habituation. Manufactured emotions are described as the product of conscious appraisals about why the trauma occurred and the implications of those appraisals on here-and-now cognitions (i.e., assimilation and overaccommodation of trauma-related material). Take the case of a natural disaster survivor who believes that the outcomes of the disaster occurred because he or others did not do enough to protect himself and his family (self- or other-blame); he is likely to feel ongoing guilt and/or anger and be distrustful of himself or others. In this way, appraisals are manufacturing ongoing negative emotions that will be maintained as long as he continues to think in this manner. Flowing from this theory, cognitive interventions aimed at changing the maladaptive appraisals (i.e., assimilation) and consequences of the appraisals (i.e., overaccommodation) to more balanced beliefs (i.e., accommodation) about the trauma and its consequences will lead to changes in the manufactured emotions.

CASE EXAMPLE USING BEHAVIORAL AND COGNITIVE CONCEPTUALIZATIONS

In Table 1.1, we present the case of a survivor of a school shooting and offer both behavioral and cognitive conceptualizations of what has prevented her natural recovery and that would inform treatment interventions.

Table 1.1

Case Conceptualization According to Emotional Processing Theory and Social Cognitive Theory

Case description	Conceptualization using emotional processing theory	Conceptualization using social cognitive theory
Cindy, a 19-year-old undergraduate student presented for treatment 6 months following a school shooting at her university. Although she was not injured during the shooting, she witnessed many of her peers get shot, and several of them resultantly died. Cindy explained the she was in a large lecture hall when a masked shooter entered the room and began firing at random. The shooter then selected specific individuals, lined them up, and began executing them. By hiding behind a row of seats near the back of the lecture hall, Cindy was able to	*Traumatic event causes the development of a maladaptive fear structure.*	*Appraisals about the traumatic event are influenced by preexisting positive or negative beliefs about self, others, and the world. The trauma also impacts these beliefs.*

(continued)

	Table 1.1	
Case Conceptualization According to Emotional Processing Theory and Social Cognitive Theory (*Continued*)		
Case description	Conceptualization using emotional processing theory	Conceptualization using social cognitive theory

remain out of sight until the shooter left the lecture hall and proceeded to fire at random in the hallways of the building before he eventually took his own life.		
In the weeks following the shooting, Cindy continued to think about the events that transpired and experienced emotional and physiological distress when she was reminded of the trauma. She explained that several types of reminders would trigger these reactions, such as having people ask about the shooting, seeing it reported in the news, having to return to the her classes, and thinking about the event. She would do everything that she could to keep the event out of her mind. She refused to talk to anyone about what had happened and about what she was going through. Eventually, Cindy's distress became too much for her to tolerate and she began making drastic efforts to avoid trauma reminders. She refused to go to her classes and eventually dropped out of her undergraduate program. Her fear began to generalize, and she reported fear and anxiety when in situations similar to, or that reminded her of, the shooting (e.g., going to movie theaters, hearing about gun violence).	*Incomplete processing of the trauma due to escape behaviors and avoidance of trauma-related cues, which serve to reinforce the fear structure and maintain the symptoms of PTSD.*	*Natural emotions related to the traumatic event are avoided. Manufactured feelings result from problematic trauma appraisals. Reminders in the environment are also avoided, which maintains beliefs that are disrupted as a result of the trauma and maladaptive appraisals.*
In the assessment, Cindy reported that she should have done more to prevent the shooter from killing the individuals he picked out in the lecture hall by pulling a fire alarm. She also expressed a belief that the school should have done more to monitor for guns on campus. Finally, one of her best friends died in the shooting, and Cindy was experiencing survivor guilt.		*Maladaptive trauma appraisals cause and maintain PTSD symptoms.*

CONCLUSION

A strong understanding of the theories underlying behavioral and cognitive interventions for PTSD is critical to efficient and effective treatment provision. Behavioral interventions are grounded in classic learning models of anxiety, with more recent innovations including cognitive structures that store information about the traumatic event. Cognitive interventions are based in cognitive models of psychopathology that include beliefs about the self, others, and the world more generally that guide interpretation of traumatic events and the consequences of events on these beliefs. By understanding the theories underlying cognitive and behavioral interventions, clinicians can individually tailor the delivery of these techniques for clients with different presentations and comorbidities to provide optimal treatment for PTSD.

2

Trauma-Focused Interventions: Behavioral Techniques and Treatment Packages

As discussed in Chapter 1, classic behavioral theory of posttraumatic stress disorder (PTSD) posits that a traumatic event elicits an initial fear response that can subsequently be elicited by stimuli (i.e., images, people, sensory experiences) present during or associated with the traumatic event (Foa & Kozak, 1986; Litz & Keane, 1989). In this way, classical conditioning processes account for the onset of symptoms. Maladaptive responses to these trauma-related cues, and namely avoidance, contribute to the maintenance of the disorder. In fact, active attempts to suppress or distract oneself from trauma-related material often result in the increased salience and frequency of the material itself, thus increasing the reexperiencing symptoms of PTSD (Beck, Gudmundsdottir, Palyo, Miller, & Grant, 2006; Wenzlaff & Wegner, 2000). The escape or avoidance response that individuals with PTSD engage in when confronted with reexperiencing

http://dx.doi.org/10.1037/14372-003
Treating PTSD With Cognitive-Behavioral Therapies: Interventions That Work, by C. M. Monson and P. Shnaider

symptoms prevents the processing of the traumatic event and does not allow them to learn that trauma-related reminders no longer pose a threat (Foa & Kozak, 1986). For example, if a survivor of a motor vehicle accident began to avoid driving or being in automobiles altogether, he or she would never have the opportunity to learn that simply being in a car does not necessarily result in getting into an accident. Thus, the goals of trauma-focused behavioral interventions for PTSD are to present trauma-related material to the client and allow him or her to habituate to the distress associated with these cues, as well as to allow the client to gain new, more adaptive, information about the perceived threat or danger associated with these cues.

This chapter describes two of the most common trauma-focused behavioral interventions for PTSD—imaginal and in vivo exposure—and provides case examples to illustrate their delivery. These are followed by an overview of prolonged exposure (Foa, Hembree, & Rothbaum, 2007), the best-validated behavioral treatment package for the treatment of PTSD. Finally, common problems associated with delivering trauma-focused behavioral interventions for PTSD are described.

OVERVIEW OF KEY INTERVENTIONS

The overall goal of the behavioral interventions described in this section is to change behavior and emotions, which have been found to also change trauma-related cognitions (Foa & Rauch, 2004). *Imaginal* and *in vivo* exposure techniques are the mainstay behavioral interventions used in the treatment of PTSD.

Imaginal Exposure

Although the memory of a traumatic event is not harmful in and of itself, recalling the memory can elicit strong emotions encoded with it, such as fear and anxiety. As a result, individuals with PTSD tend to make efforts to avoid thinking about or remembering the trauma and the associated emotions. Such efforts reduce short-term discomfort and distress; however, engaging in behavior aimed at avoiding traumatic memories prevents individuals with PTSD from learning that memories of the trauma are safe. Facing the memory, and not becoming distracted from and not avoiding its recollection, ultimately reduces the distress associated with the memory in the longer term.

Imaginal exposure has routinely and safely been used as a behavioral intervention for a range of anxiety disorders, as well as PTSD (Antony & Swinson, 2000; Rothbaum, 2006). This technique involves systematically exposing a client to a feared stimulus with the goal of reducing the subjective fear or anxiety caused by the stimulus. With respect to PTSD, imaginal exposure is used to expose a client to his or her encoded memory of traumatic events. In this way, the client's phobic response is to the memory of the traumatic experience.

Imaginal exposure in the treatment of PTSD has several aims. These include habituation to the fear elicited by the trauma memory and induction of new learning. Specifically, imaginal exposure aims to reduce the automatic fear response that is elicited in the presence of the memory of the traumatic event, as well as to allow the client to incorporate new information about his or her ability to tolerate fear and cope in the presence of the traumatic memory. The former takes place through the process of habituation and the latter via the incorporation of new information that alters the client's beliefs about the traumatic event (Foa et al., 2007; Lyons & Keane, 1989). The process of repeatedly imagining the event in as much detail as possible, while not allowing escape and avoidance behaviors, provides competing and incompatible responses to the conditioned association between the trauma memory and fear response, leading to the alteration of the fear associated with the memory and the reduction of PTSD symptoms (Foa & Kozak, 1986).

In Vivo Exposure

Similar to the fear brought on by memories of the traumatic event, external stimuli in the environment, such as people, places, objects, and situations associated with the trauma, can also cue or trigger fear. These need not be inherently dangerous or threatening, yet due to a client's interpretation of what these cues signify, as well as their associations with the client's distress, these reminders begin to automatically signal fear in the client and motivate her or him to engage in escape or avoidant behavior. As discussed earlier, escape and avoidance are associated with short-term relief from the distress brought on by the feared cue. However, this behavior prevents the client from gaining new, adaptive information about the feared cue and, in fact, promotes the maintenance of PTSD by reinforcing the notion that the trauma-related distress represents important information that must be reacted to.

Like imaginal exposures, in vivo exposures are a staple of behavioral treatments across the anxiety disorders (Abramowitz, Deacon, & Whiteside, 2010) and involve systematically exposing a client to feared people, places, situations, and objects currently in her or his environment. Through this process, clients learn to break the pattern of negative reinforcement of their fear, habituate to their fear response, learn new information about the cues and their ability to cope with their anxiety or fear, and correct unrealistic predictions about what results from being in the presence of a trauma-related cue (Foa et al., 2007; Foa & Kozak, 1986). In addition, clients gain mastery and control over their fears (Başoğlu, Şalcioğlu, Livanou, Kalender, & Acar, 2005).

Within the context of PTSD treatment, in vivo exposures are used to address and approach avoided stimuli that trigger trauma-related thoughts or memories. These might include men of a certain build or ethnicity for someone who was sexually assaulted, driving or riding in a car for those who experienced motor vehicle accidents, or loud or crowded places for those who have experienced or witnessed combat traumas.

Although the content or feared stimuli may differ from client to client, the principles of conducting in vivo exposures remain consistent. The goal is to expose the client to objectively safe but feared situations until the fear subsides. During this process, clients also learn to correct or disprove beliefs or predictions that they hold about potential negative outcomes of being in the presence of the feared stimulus as well as their ability to cope with distress.

APPLYING BEHAVIORAL TECHNIQUES

There are several key techniques used in behavioral treatments for PTSD. These include education about the Subjective Units of Distress Scale (SUDS; Wolpe, 1969), imaginal exposures, and in vivo exposures.

Subjective Units of Distress Scale

Before engaging in imaginal or in vivo exposures with a client, it is important to introduce the SUDS. The SUDS serves two key purposes. First, it allows clients to express and convey the amount of distress they are experiencing at any given time during an imaginal or in vivo exposure. This is critical for tracking their distress or fear reduction during the exposure. Second, and specific to in vivo exposures, the SUDS allows clients to quantify and gauge the fear associated with each object or situation to be confronted, in order to develop an exposure hierarchy. Exposure hierarchies are discussed below (see the section on conducting an in vivo exposure).

Regardless of the exposure technique to be used, the SUDS can be introduced in the same manner. Put simply, the SUDS is a measure of how much distress, fear, anxiety, or other negative emotion clients feel at any given moment, or how much distress they anticipate a given situation will cause them. The scale ranges from 0 to 100, with increasing values signifying increasing distress. Given that the scale is subjective, each client will have different ratings of how much distress a given situation causes him or her. Thus, it is helpful for clients to develop points of reference so that they can understand that there is a range of distressing situations. This may be particularly helpful when working with a client who tends to give all situations a SUDS rating of 100. Take, for example, the SUDS reference points developed by a survivor of a motor vehicle accident, a survivor of combat trauma, and a survivor of a sexual assault (see Figure 2.1).

Some clinicians prefer to use the terms *fear, anxiety*, or *distress* more generally rather than talking about the SUDS specifically. The purpose of the SUDS is not to label the emotion but rather for the therapist and client to have a shorthand method of communication to gauge how the client is doing and whether the exposure needs to be modified. Irrespective of

Traumatic Event: Motor Vehicle Accident

```
0------------------25------------------50------------------75------------------100
At home          Taking Public        Being the          Driving on a       Driving on the
relaxing         transportation       passenger in a     low-traffic        highway
                                      car                street
```

Traumatic Event: Combat

```
0------------------25------------------50------------------75------------------100
At home      Sitting far from an exit     Being          Watching         At a crowded
relaxing     at a theater                 reminded of    Fireworks        mall/feeling like
                                          the traumatic                   I'm back in combat
                                          event
```

Traumatic Event: Sexual Assault

```
0------------------25------------------50------------------75------------------100
At home          Watching the news     Walking alone    Going to a bar    Walking alone at
relaxing                               during the day                     night
```

Figure 2.1

Examples of SUDS reference points.

what you wish to call it, introducing some method of gauging distress is crucial to the exposure process.

Conducting Imaginal Exposure in Session

When conducting an imaginal exposure, therapists typically ask clients to close their eyes and imagine themselves back in the traumatic event. Clients are then asked to recount the traumatic experience in as much detail as possible, with a specific focus on sensory details. They should recount the event in first-person, present tense in order to elicit the memory as vividly and carefully as possible.

It is imperative that clients not simply retell the story of the traumatic experience but, rather, fully engage with the memory. This important difference needs to be understood when conducting imaginal exposures. Essentially, retelling a story involves relaying the facts of what happened during the traumatic event. This can be equated to that given for a court proceeding or a police report. Typically, there is a sense of emotional detachment when retelling the memory in this way. Full engagement with the memory, as is necessary for imaginal exposure, involves more than just a factual retelling; clients should also engage with the emotions they felt at the time of the event and allow themselves to experience those emotions during the exposure.

In addition, sensory details such as sounds and smells that were present during the event should also be integrated into the exposure. This will allow the client to better engage with the emotions associated with the memory, as well as provide a more vivid memory with which to work. For example, a motor vehicle accident survivor may focus on the sound of the car colliding upon impact, the smell of spilled gasoline, and the fear that he experienced when another car swerved into his lane. Similarly, a survivor of childhood sexual abuse may express emotions such as guilt for feeling special or finding pleasure in the abuse they experienced, as well as shame and fear about family members overhearing the ongoing abuse. They may also focus on sensory details such as things that the abuser said to them or details about how the abuser smelled and looked.

Although client engagement with the traumatic memory is necessary, it is important that the client recognize that the event is not happening again in the present moment. Instead, the client should be aware that he or she is experiencing the memory in a safe environment and that exposure to the memory poses no current threat. In fact, increasing a client's ability to differentiate between the memory of the traumatic event and the experience of being retraumatized (i.e., feeling as though the traumatic event is happening again and that the same negative outcomes that occurred at the time of the traumatic event will happen again) is among the goals of imaginal exposure (Foa et al., 2007). Therapists with clients who struggle with this distinction will likely evidence signs of over- or under-engagement during imaginal exposures, and thus may benefit from the suggestions presented below (see the sections in this chapter on over- and under-engagement and related reactions). Although suggested guidelines regarding the length of the exposure differ across studies and treatment protocols, they are expected to last for about 45 to 60 minutes or until the client has experienced a significant reduction in his or her anxiety (Bryant, Moulds, Guthrie, Dang, & Nixon, 2003; Foa et al., 2007; Keane, Fairbank, Caddell, & Zimfring, 1989; Zayfert & Becker, 2007). Thus, it may be helpful to schedule 90-minute sessions when conducting in-session imaginal exposures.

In early sessions of imaginal exposure, clients may offer a briefer rendition of the traumatic memory. If the client finishes recounting the experience before the prescribed time elapses, the exercise should be repeated until the end of the allotted time. As with most behavioral interventions, repetition is essential to achieving successful outcomes. Some have suggested eight or more in-session imaginal exposures plus those done for homework (Foa et al., 2007); however, in clinical research studies, imaginal exposures have ranged from as few as four to as many as 16 (Boudewyns & Hyer, 1990; Bryant et al., 2003; Keane et al., 1989; Richards, Lovell, & Marks, 1994; Tarrier, Pilgrim, et al., 1999). Yet others have suggested using clinical judgment in determining the number of imaginal exposures to be conducted (Cooper & Clum, 1989; Zayfert & Becker, 2007). Clinical judgment should be based on changes in the client's ability to tolerate the exposure, the degree to which the memory elicits fear or anxiety, as well as the length of time needed for the anxiety to subside through the exposure.

During an imaginal exposure, it is important for the therapist to assume a nonintrusive stance in order to avoid distracting the client or any other behavior that may cause disengagement with the traumatic memory. However, it is important to establish a balance between being nonintrusive and maintaining a supportive atmosphere during these sessions. Using specific and well-placed statements can encourage the client to stay engaged with the trauma memory, especially if she or he attempts to avoid distressing elements of the traumatic memory. As clients become more experienced with imaginal exposures, they generally require fewer prompts by the therapist and are better able to engage with and focus on the most distressing elements of the traumatic event.

In addition to avoiding distraction from the traumatic memory, the therapist's role during an imaginal exposure is to monitor the client's subjective distress and engagement with traumatic material. It is typically recommended that the therapist ask about a client's subjective distress every 5 minutes (Foa et al., 2007; Zayfert & Becker, 2007). Asking clients to rate how vivid the memory is or how engaged they are with the memory may also be helpful in ensuring that they are maximally benefiting from the exposure. Clients' reported subjective distress also provides information as to how engaged they are with the memory.

Graphing a client's distress ratings throughout the imaginal exposure is also helpful. This can be done by designing a graph with *time* on the *x*-axis and *SUDS* on the *y*-axis, which allows client and therapist to see how the client's distress changes across the exposure. This information can be presented to the client upon the conclusion of the exercise. Consistent with the goals of imaginal exposure, concrete graphing of distress reduction across the session provides clients with additional information on their ability to tolerate distress (integration of new information), as well as the fact that their fear response is reduced with continued exposure to the trauma memory (habituation to the distress associated with trauma memory).

Inquiring about and recording a client's distress will also help therapists identify hot spots. *Hot spots* are the segments of the traumatic memory that are most distressing to the client. Often clients will have difficulty talking about these parts of the memory or may show signs of physiological or psychological distress when recounting them. Researchers have shown that hot spots tend to be the elements of a traumatic memory that occur most often as part of a client's reexperiencing symptoms (i.e., they appear in flashbacks, intrusive thoughts, and images; Grey & Holmes, 2008; Holmes, Grey, & Young, 2005). When conducting imaginal exposures, therapists should identify hot spots during the first few renditions of the memory. Asking clients if specific parts of their memories are particularly difficult for them may also help therapists identify hot spots.

With repeated imaginal exposures being completed throughout treatment sessions, a therapist should transition a client's focus to the hot spots. This can be done by asking the client to slow down during the recounting of these portions of the memory to provide increased detail about the sensory stimuli present at that moment, and to engage with emotions that the client felt at the time or are currently feeling. Given that hot spots are considered the most feared elements of imaginal exposures, therapists should ensure that clients habituate to these parts of the memory and that they are not rushing through them or disengaging in order to minimize their distress. If this proves difficult, therapists should consider conducting repeated imaginal exposures of a hot spot on its own before continuing with the remainder of the memory.

Imaginal exposure exercises should also be conducted both within and outside of therapy sessions to maximize their effectiveness. Typically, therapy sessions are conducted weekly or twice-weekly until the recounting of the traumatic event no longer elicits a fear or anxiety response (Bryant et al., 2003; Cooper & Clum, 1989; Richards et al., 1994). Listening to recordings of in-session imaginal exposures is common practice in PTSD treatment (Foa et al., 2007; Richards et al., 1994). Thus, imaginal exposures conducted in session should be recorded for the client to listen to daily between sessions. This aids in the processing of the trauma and the reduction of the fear response. Repeated recounting of the traumatic event and listening to recorded versions of the imaginal exposure weakens the conditioned association between the traumatic memory and the related fear response through the integration of new information and habituation to the fear elicited by the trauma memory.

Upon the conclusion of each exposure, the therapist and client should engage in brief processing or debriefing. This provides an opportunity for the client to describe his or her experience and for the therapist to reinforce the client for engaging in this difficult task. It is particularly helpful to show clients a visual depiction of their reduction in distress ratings across the exposure in order to highlight their improvement and encourage them to listen to the recordings of the in-session imaginal exposure daily outside of session.

Case Example: Terry

Terry, a 42-year-old earthquake survivor, had been experiencing PTSD symptoms for over 8 years. Terry consistently avoided thoughts and images related to witnessing the injuries and deaths of others during the earthquake. Throughout the years, he began spending an increasing amount of time at work and filling his days with hobbies and activities. By the time he sought treatment, Terry had managed to fill his entire week with various obligations in order to keep his mind occupied and to minimize the possibility that he would think about the traumatic event. He also worked hard to convince others that the earthquake had not affected him. He did this by avoiding people that knew he had gone through this experience and by quickly changing the topic when it came up. However, he found that whenever he had free time, he would have unwanted intrusive thoughts and images about the earthquake. In addition, he was having increasingly distressing nightmares that were causing him to lose several hours of sleep each night. His repeated violent awakenings throughout the night had also disturbed his wife's sleep, resulting in them no longer sharing a bedroom. Terry found that the harder he worked to avoid these thoughts, the more frequent they would become, and that they were getting stronger each day. He feared that if he thought about the memory he would lose control of his emotions and would not be able to cope. He was concerned that the fear and panic that occurred when he was reminded of the trauma would last forever. By avoiding thoughts about the memory, he never allowed himself to test out his predictions. Furthermore, through his repeated avoidance of the trauma memory, his fear continued to grow.

Terry eventually sought treatment because his symptoms were significantly impairing his work and family life. After receiving a thorough assessment of his PTSD and comorbid symptoms, psychoeducation about PTSD symptoms, and a rationale for using imaginal exposures, Terry received a number of sessions of imaginal exposure. With encouragement from his therapist, he engaged with the trauma memory in session by providing a detailed account of what he witnessed during the earthquake. The therapist prompted him to begin the account at the point at which he initially was aware that the earthquake was happening. She prompted him to describe in detail where he was at the time, who he was with, what he saw, how it ended, the sensations he had, and importantly, what he was thinking and feeling at the time. With each recounting, the therapist asked Terry to provide even more sensory and emotional details about the experience to facilitate habituation to the memory and to increase his mastery of his anxiety related to facing it. These retellings were recorded so that Terry could listen to the account outside of session for homework.

By engaging with the memory in a systematic manner and not allowing himself to escape or avoid it, he recognized that his fear and anxiety subsided as the exposures went on. Furthermore, he was able to test some of the predictions he had made about what would happen if he allowed himself to think about the trauma. He recognized that he could fully maintain control of his emotions and that, although he felt fear and anxiety throughout the exposure, these feelings quickly passed. Through the use of repeated imaginal exposures, Terry slowly began to feel more conformable with discussing the trauma and telling people about his experience. He no longer feared the memory and was able to recognize that the memory itself was not dangerous.

Excerpt From an In-Session Imaginal Exposure

The following case example is an excerpt from an imaginal exposure with a client who was in a motor vehicle accident with his wife and young child, in which his child was killed. Although only part of the exposure is provided, when conducting imaginal exposures in session, the exposure should be conducted until the end of the memory and repeated for at least 45 to 60 minutes. The example below was the first imaginal exposure conducted with this client. With the first exposure it is common for a client's SUDS rating to be elevated throughout the entire memory. With repetition during the session, as well as across several sessions, the memory will elicit lower distress ratings and it will take a shorter duration to have the distress rating reduce across the exposure.

Therapist: Let's start by having you close your eyes and sit comfortably in your chair. I'd like you to go back to the memory of what happened during the accident. Try to talk about it as if you were back in the moment or as if it were happening right now. Remember to talk in first person and not as if you were watching the event take place from another person's perspective. You may experience a number of strong emotions, but I want you to remember that it is just a memory and that a memory itself can't cause you any harm. You are safe here in the office. The memory alone isn't dangerous. During the exposure I'm going to ask you how distressed you are using the SUDS ratings. Try to tell me as quickly as you can and go right back into the memory. If you feel overly afraid or anxious, you may open your eyes, but try to stay with the memory. However, do your best to keep them closed throughout the exposure. During the exposure I won't be speaking much, except to help keep you moving forward. We will talk about it when you are done. Are you ready to start?

Client: Yes.

Therapist: What is your SUDS just before we start?

Client: 80.

Therapist: Okay. Take yourself back to the day of the accident. What happened just before?

Client: I am driving home from visiting my brother-in-law and his family. It is getting dark and it is drizzling. It's hard to see the lines dividing my lane from oncoming traffic. I'm looking in my rearview mirror to check on my son who is falling asleep in his car seat. My wife is sitting beside me and asking me about something that her brother had said to me while she was in the kitchen. I'm looking in the rearview mirror again and I see a car. It's coming toward us extremely fast. Its high beams are on and it's flashing them at me. Now I see another car just behind it. They keep on cutting each other off. They are getting very close to my car and are trying to pass me. I try to move over to let them pass, but there is no shoulder on the road for me to slow down or pull onto. My wife is very nervous. She turns to look out the rear windshield. I'm shaking and I don't know what to do. The cars are very close now. They are just behind me to the right. They are trying to squeeze past me on the right side, between me and the guardrail.

I try to let them pass by moving a bit into the oncoming traffic lane. Their high beams are hitting my mirror and making it hard for me to see.

Therapist: What's your SUDS rating?

Client: 100. They are finally passing me on my right side. My wife is screaming at me to move over. I hear a loud horn. My car is still partly in the oncoming traffic lane . . . (The client pauses for a number of seconds.)

Therapist: You're doing great. Keep going.

Client: The second car is now passing and I hear the horn again. It's loud. Like a big truck. I still can't see very well and I'm sweating. My wife is saying something to me but I can't make out what she is saying. The horn is getting louder and it keeps sounding over and over again. Even with the second car passing me, something is still blinding me. I realize that it is a truck coming toward us and that I'm in its way because I moved into its lane. I try to swerve back into my lane, but it is too late. (The client, now visibly distressed, is having trouble continuing. He is crying and shaking his head back and forth, as if saying "no".)

Therapist: Remember, it's just a memory. You are safe here in the office; keep going.

Client: The truck hits us on the back left side door, the seat where my son was sitting. (The client is sweating and becoming tearful.)

Therapist: I know this is hard, but stay with the memory. (The therapist notes this section of the memory as a potential hot spot. The client pauses for a few more seconds and then continues.)

Client: I hear a loud crash. The car is spinning violently. My wife keeps screaming and the car keeps spinning. I can't see anything and all I hear is my wife's screaming. The car finally stops. I'm bleeding from my left arm and the window is broken. I look at my wife beside me and she is crying. I ask her if she is hurt. She says no. We simultaneously look at the backseat to check on our son. His car seat is turned in the backseat and he is lying sideways in it. His body is twisted in the car seat. He isn't moving and he isn't breathing. He isn't making a sound. I'm screaming for my wife to call

911, but she is just sitting there sobbing. I crawl over the seat and now I'm in the backseat with my son. I want to hold him but I know I shouldn't move him. I fumble to find my cell phone in my pocket and call 911. The dispatch operator answers almost immediately. She asks if I need fire-fighters, an ambulance, or the police, but I can't answer. I am crying and I keep repeating, "It was an accident." My wife is screaming now. She keeps on saying, "My baby is dead, my baby is dead." The dispatch operator asks for my location. I tell her I'm just east of Exit 92 heading west on the I90. She tells me that help is on the way. She's now asking me to check on the baby. I tell her that he's not breathing and she tells me not to touch him and that the ambulance will be there soon. I can hear sirens. The sound is getting louder and louder. It sounds as if there are 100 police cars heading toward us. The police and paramedics arrive. They take my wife and I to the back of an ambulance and turn us so we can't see our car. The para-medics ask us if we are okay. I tell them we are fine, but my wife can't stop crying. She is shaking and screaming. The paramedics see the cut on my arm and start to treat it. They tell me that it isn't too deep and that I won't need stiches. I keep asking about my baby, but the paramedics won't give me a response. Finally, I see a police officer begin to move toward us. (The client pauses. He is tearful.)

Therapist: You're doing great; what happened next?

Client: The police officer looks stoic. His face looks flat. He looks at my wife and I and says that he is very sorry. Our son did not survive the crash. My wife begins to scream again, "My baby is dead, my baby is dead." Her crying seems out of control and the paramedics try to comfort her. I look at the officer with a blank stare and ask him what I'm supposed to do. I can't feel anything. I feel empty. I know I'm supposed to cry, supposed to feel sad, supposed to feel something, but all I can do is ask the police officer what I'm supposed to do. The officer gives me the address of the hospital where my son is being taken and gives me instructions on how to claim his body from the morgue. I thank the police officer. He then asks me what happened. I tell him about the cars that were racing and the oncom-ing truck. The police officer takes my statement. He tells me that the truck driver was injured and taken to the hospital. I finish giving him my statement. Another police officer comes and asks my wife for her statement. She has calmed down by now. She returns to where I am sitting, on the back of the ambulance but doesn't say anything. A police officer tells us that he will take care of getting us home. We get into his car, I give him our address and none of us speak for the entire ride.

Therapist: What's your SUDS rating?

Client: 70.

Therapist: I know how hard that was for you. You did a great job, and I appreciate you sharing that memory with me. I know at times it feels tough, but it will get easier each time.

Client: I didn't think I was going to be able to continue.

Therapist: Sometimes it can feel that way, but it's important to keep going. Remember, it is just a memory, and a memory on its own can't hurt you. As we keep practicing these exposures you will feel less fear and anxiety. Eventually the memory will no longer cause you any fear. You should be really proud of what you just did. It took a lot of courage to talk about the accident so openly. How do you feel?

Client: I feel okay. A little anxious still.

Therapist: Do you think you could try that again?

Client: I think so.

Therapist: Okay, when you are ready, I want you to start again.

Conducting In Vivo Exposures

Exposure Hierarchy

To prepare for in vivo exposures, a client and therapist first work collaboratively to develop an *exposure hierarchy*. An exposure hierarchy is a rank-ordered list of feared stimuli to which the client will eventually expose himself or herself. The hierarchy does not need to be exhaustive, but it should represent a sample of the trauma-related cues or triggers and avoided situations. We recommend picking between 10 and 15 items to place on the hierarchy. Typically these hierarchies consist of a variety of feared objects, people, places, situations, and activities; they need to be individually customized for each client.

In developing a list of currently feared objects, people, places, situations, and activities, the client and therapist proceed to rate the subjective distress associated with each item using the SUDS. Then, the items are organized from lowest to highest SUDS rating, creating the exposure hierarchy that will guide the in vivo exposures. For those items with particularly high SUDS ratings, we recommend developing smaller or more graded exposures that approximate the larger, more distressing stimulus. In other words, the item would be divided into smaller or more manageable steps with lower SUDS ratings. Using the example of a woman who was sexually assaulted in a parking lot, this patient assigned *going to a parking lot* a SUDS rating of 80, which felt too overwhelming and led her to hesitate in approaching this situation. In this case, a graded approach is strongly recommended. Accordingly, the therapist and client worked together to break down the exposure (e.g., going to a parking lot during the day with a trusted companion [SUDS = 50], going to a parking lot during the day alone [SUDS = 60], going to a parking lot at night with a trusted companion [SUDS = 70], going to a parking lot at night alone [SUDS = 80]). This graded approach allows clients to recognize that there are steps along the way to conquering the items with high SUDS ratings on their hierarchies. In addition, the confidence gained along the way by conquering the items with lower SUDS ratings may provide additional motivation to attempt and work through the more difficult ones. When conducting in vivo exposures, it is important that clients are objectively safe (see section below on safety during in vivo exposures). Exhibit 2.2 shows an exposure hierarchy of an individual who witnessed a suicide. Note the variation and gradation of difficulty in the types of the exposures.

Standard practice in utilizing *in vivo* exposure is to begin with an item that has a moderate SUDS rating. Although recommendations regarding an exact starting point differ, most treatments suggest beginning with an item rated between 40 and 50 on the SUDS (Foa et al., 2007; Zayfert

Exhibit 2.2	
Example of an In Vivo Exposure Hierarchy	
Traumatic Event: Witnessing Someone Jump Into the Subway	
Objects, People, Places, Situations, and Activities	**SUDS**
Imagining someone jumping while on the platform	100
Imagining someone jumping while riding the subway	90
Watching a film in which someone jumps into the subway	85
Looking at people on the platform as the subway arrives	80
Watching the tracks as subway trains pull into the station	70
Standing on a subway platform alone at rush hour	55
Standing on a subway platform alone	50
Standing on a subway platform with a friend at rush hour	35
Standing on a subway platform with a friend	30
Taking public transportation	20

Note. SUDS = Subjective Units of Distress Scale.

& Becker, 2007). This ensures that the fear response will be activated, a requirement for the successful treatment of PTSD as per behavioral theory (Foa & Kozak, 1986), and also protects against overwhelming the client, which could potentially deter clients from engaging in future exposures. As with imaginal exposures, therapists (or clients) should monitor the SUDS ratings every 5 minutes during the exposures, monitoring for reductions throughout the exposure. The client's subjective distress should also be graphed, and this may be helpful in providing the client with additional information about his or her response to the feared stimuli.

With repeated in vivo exposure, the fear response associated with the stimuli is mastered, allowing the client to proceed up the hierarchy to their next-most-feared item over the course of therapy. Repetition of exposures is essential to gaining mastery of each feared situation; thus, completion of exposures outside of session is critical to successful treatment outcomes. In addition, it is recommended that clients periodically re-rate items on their exposure hierarchies in order to evaluate their progress and reevaluate the fear associated with each item.

Table 2.1 contains principles for successful in vivo exposures.

Case Example: Brenda

Brenda, a 17-year-old high school student, had been raped at a party 6 months ago and was recently diagnosed with PTSD. After experiencing her traumatic event, Brenda became increasingly isolated. Although many of her friends had known that she had been raped, she began spending less time with them. At first she made efforts to avoid going to parties, specifically if there was alcohol present. However, over time, Brenda began avoiding parties altogether, and eventually any large group of people. This included going to malls, taking public transportation, and even attending school. Brenda reported that when she saw men who looked like the man who had raped her, she would experience a panic attack. Furthermore, she would find the experience of seeing men who looked like the perpetrator so disturbing that it was easier to avoid people altogether. Brenda was concerned that being in the presence of these men might put her at risk for another assault. She was convinced that all men were bad and that she could never be safe in their presence.

During the course of Brenda's treatment, she engaged in a number of in vivo exposures. She began by going to the mall with her mother for several hours each evening. At first, the sight of any man dramatically increased her anxiety. However, by staying in the situation, she noticed that her anxiety began to decrease. Through repeated daily exposures conducted at the mall, Brenda was eventually able to go into the mall alone and even interact with male store clerks. She was able to counter her initial belief that all men were bad and to recognize that simply being in the presence of men did not increase the likelihood of her being assaulted. As treatment progressed, Brenda conducted a variety of exposures, including returning to school, getting together with male friends, and eventually

Table 2.1
Guidelines for Successful In Vivo Exposures

Guideline	Things to remember
Plan	Lay out a solid rationale.
	Plan each exposure collaboratively with the client.
	The client should be fully aware of and committed to the exposure.
	The client should not feel coerced or obligated to engage in an exposure.
Stay in the situation	Forewarn clients that they may want to stop or abandon an exposure.
	Although exposures should not be stopped due to the client feeling overwhelmed, it is ultimately the client's choice to continue.
	Remain in the situation until fear reduction is accomplished.
	Stopping an exposure prematurely may result in continued reinforcement or worsening of the avoidance behavior.
Repeat	With repeated exposure, the subjective intensity of distress and length of time for distress to reduce will diminish.
	Each exposure provides additional corrective information that allows clients to reevaluate their beliefs about the feared object or situation.
	Repeated exposure provides the client numerous experiences of being exposed to the stimulus without the subsequent, maladaptive, avoidance behavior.
	Clients should repeat an exposure several times before moving on to a new one; daily practice is ideal.
Vary	Varying a specific trauma-related stimulus increases the likelihood of generalizing the fear reduction to other trauma-related cues.
	Varying elements of an exposure provides the client with numerous contexts in which to learn and incorporate corrective information. Consider varying: ■ where the exposure takes place ■ who the client is with at the time ■ how involved or close the client is with the feared stimulus Be creative in developing ways in which the feared stimulus can be varied.

Note. Data from Antony and Roemer (2011), Antony and Swinson (2000), and Monson and Fredman (2012).

attending a party. With each exposure, her initial fear decreased and she experienced fear reduction more rapidly. Eventually, Brenda recognized that these situations and people were not dangerous, and that being in their presence no longer caused her fear.

TRAUMA-FOCUSED BEHAVIORAL TREATMENT PACKAGE FOR PTSD: PROLONGED EXPOSURE

Although the trauma-focused behavioral interventions reviewed above can be used in isolation, these techniques are integrated in the evidence-based treatment for PTSD *prolonged exposure* (PE; Foa et al., 2007). To date, exposure therapy (usually consisting of combined imaginal and in vivo exposures) has been tested in over 10 trials, with at least eight being randomized controlled trials. The majority of these studies have been based on the prolonged exposure protocol or slight variations of said protocol (Foa, Keane, Friedman, & Cohen, 2009). As a result, exposure therapy is prescribed as a front-line treatment in several treatment guidelines (e.g., Foa et al., 2009; Management of Post-Traumatic Stress Working Group, 2010).

PE uses both imaginal and in vivo exposure techniques to address PTSD. Because these two core techniques are described in detail above, we present an overview of the PE protocol and spend more time on interventions included in PE not previously discussed (see Table 2.2).

PE is a 10-to-12-session manualized therapy comprising four key elements: psychoeducation about PTSD and the rationale for PE, breathing retraining, in vivo exposure, and imaginal exposure. Sessions are designed to be 90 minutes in length and can be delivered weekly or twice-weekly (Foa et al., 2007). Based on emotional processing theory (Foa & Kozak, 1986), which includes cognitive elements of the original behavioral conceptualization of PTSD, PE is described to assist in the processing of a traumatic event by confronting its memory and the associated trauma-related material, as well as altering maladaptive cognitions associated with trauma-related stimuli. Foa et al. (2007) equated the processing of a traumatic memory to the digestive system, whereby the discomfort of PTSD symptoms remains present until the memory is properly processed or digested. Similarly, they

Table 2.2
Session-by-Session Guide to Prolonged Exposure

Session	Key interventions	Homework
1	Treatment overview and rationale Trauma interview Breathing retraining	Review the treatment rationale Practice breathing retraining daily Listen to audio recording of the session
2	Homework review Common reactions to trauma Rationale for in vivo exposures Introduction to the SUDS Development of exposure hierarchy	Review common reactions to trauma daily Practice breathing retraining daily Review and add to exposure hierarchy Review *in vivo* exposures rationale *In vivo* exposures daily Listen to audio recording of the session
3	Homework review Rationale for imaginal exposures Imaginal exposure Imaginal exposure debriefing	Listen to audio recording of imaginal exposure daily *In vivo* exposures daily Listen to audio recording of the session
4–9 or more	Homework review Imaginal exposure • with more detail and focus on distressing aspects of the trauma as treatment progresses Imaginal exposure debriefing Review in vivo exposures	Practice breathing retraining daily Listen to audio recording of imaginal exposure daily *In vivo* exposures daily Listen to audio recording of the session
10 or final session	Homework review Imaginal exposure Imaginal exposure debriefing • with a focus on changes in imaginal exposures throughout treatment Review of skills learned in treatment Relapse prevention Ending therapy	

Note. SUDS = Subjective Units of Distress Scale. Data from Foa, Hembree, and Rothbaum (2007).

offer another analogy in which memories are likened to files stored in folders that provide information on how to behave in situations. However, due to the unexpected nature and unpredictability of traumatic events, the brain has difficulty storing the traumatic memory. As a result, this memory requires additional attention and effort for it to be properly stored. Until the memory is processed, the symptoms of PTSD continue to be present, causing distress for the client.

Psychoeducation

Psychoeducation in the PE protocol is delivered in the first two sessions and consists of informing the client about the interventions used in PE and the role of avoidance in maintaining PTSD. The notion of how PE targets avoidance through imaginal and in vivo exposures is discussed, highlighting why the PE protocol will likely lead to improvement. Reviewing the common reactions to trauma provides an opportunity to normalize some of the reactions and experiences that the client has had since the traumatic event. Examples of common reactions include reexperiencing the trauma through unwanted memories and nightmares, increased irritability and anger, avoiding trauma-related cues, problems in interpersonal relationships, experiencing emotions like guilt and shame, and having strong negative cognitions about oneself, others and the world. An additional goal of delivering psychoeducation in PE is to instill hope and confidence that PE may successfully address clients' symptoms and help them overcome PTSD.

Breathing Retraining

Breathing retraining is introduced in the first session of PE with the intention of providing the client with a skill that can be utilized to address the distress brought on by PTSD symptoms and by talking about the traumatic event. The client is first taught to breathe normally when distressed, and later to focus on extending the exhalation and slowing down the breathing overall. In addition, breathing retraining involves educating the clients about how slowing their breath and extending their exhalation will result in a relaxed response, whereas taking in deep breaths may actually activate or increase anxiety and distress.

Clients are not to use the breathing skill during exposures because it may interfere with their learning about their ability to cope with their anxiety and learning new information about the safety of the stimuli. Although the notion of breathing skills as a safety behavior has not received as much attention in the context of PTSD treatments, the clinical utility of this skill in CBT has been debated in the literature on the treatment of panic disorder (e.g., Meuret, Wilhelm, Ritz, & Roth, 2003; Schmidt et al., 2000). According to the creators of PE, breathing retraining is the least essential element of the protocol (Foa et al., 2007). The authors go as far as to say, "The breathing skill is not critical to the process and outcome of PE" (Foa et al., 2007, p. 2). We suggest teaching the skill and letting clients make their own decisions about using it. However, we strongly discourage its use during exposures. Exposures should be conducted with full engagement and without the use of safety signals or techniques to ensure that clients learn that they can overcome the anxiety and need not rely on safety strategies in order to do so.

COMMON CHALLENGES IN DOING TRAUMA-FOCUSED BEHAVIORAL INTERVENTIONS

Each client presents with his or her own idiosyncratic factors that may facilitate or pose challenges to the delivery of behavioral interventions. However, some common problems or challenges arise when using behavioral interventions for PTSD. Below, we review some of them and discuss methods by which to address them. Having a strong therapeutic relationship with your client is key, and recognizing that each client will have unique reactions and experiences during these exercises is also critical. In addition, one should never underestimate the utility of delivering a strong and clear rationale for the use of each technique. Having clients understand the logic behind a given intervention may increase the likelihood that they complete it properly.

Overengagement and Related Reactions

Overengagement occurs when a client becomes overly distressed, emotionally flooded, or too physiologically activated during an exposure, which can lead to a number of reactions. Although reactions to overengagement may take a variety of forms, we highlight some of the more common presentations that may occur in clinical practice, including emotional numbing, dissociation, and strong physical and psychological reactions.

Although emotional numbing and dissociation are different from more active strategies to avoid trauma memories and reminders, they serve the same escape function as these efforts in maintaining PTSD symptoms. Thus, dissociation and numbing during an exposure prevent clients from fully engaging and pose barriers to new learning. The following strategies can be useful in engaging in exposures with clients who are highly dissociative or emotionally numb.

One strategy for managing these responses is to reduce the intensity of exposures to cope with distressing situations. For imaginal exposures, this may include the client keeping his or her eyes open or recounting the memory with less sensory detail. Grounding techniques, such as having the client describe the qualities of the therapist's office or physiological sensations that he or she is experiencing while sitting in the chair, may also assist in keeping the client present and engaged with the exposure. To combat emotional numbing, the therapist might also have the client describe the emotional experience or physiological sensations that he or she is experiencing. For in vivo exposures, the therapist can assign items lower on the exposure hierarchy or consider dividing existing items on the hierarchy into more manageable exposures. These strategies are intended to allow the client to focus on their anxiety and not dissociate or become emotionally numb during the exposure. Reiterating the rationale for exposure therapy may be particularly useful for motivating clients to avoid these passive escape strategies.

Strong physical reactions are also possible when working with clients who overengage during exposures. In these cases, a client may be concerned that he or she will vomit, lose continence, sweat excessively, feel nauseated, or experience other strong reactions. We encourage therapists to validate these concerns and reassure clients that if any of these things happen, it will not bother the therapist. Should a client actually have a strong reaction during an exposure, it is important to normalize the experience. Highlight that sometimes our bodies react in different ways when we are distressed or anxious, but continue to ensure that the client has a positive therapeutic experience and an opportunity for new learning through the experience of being able to cope with and overcome the distress.

Similarly, a client may display a strong psychological reaction during exposure therapy. However, it is important to differentiate between strong psychological reactions or distress and having a client with a safety concern. For example, strong psychological reactions or distress during exposures may take the form of crying, having a panic attack, or becoming very emotionally upset or dysregulated. Strong psychological reactions are not in and of themselves problematic, and therapists should not fear continuing with exposures in the presence of these reactions. However, although this happens rarely, increased psychological distress can translate into a client safety concern. For example, a client with a history of suicidality may begin to experience increased, active suicidal ideation or threaten to commit suicide. Similarly, a client with a history of self-harming behavior may report the urge or actually cut herself in order to complete exposure practice at home. In these cases, the client's safety should always take priority. It is necessary to address the safety concern, but it may or may not be necessary to stop the exposure interventions. Suicidal and self-harming behavior can serve an escape function when patients are emotionally distressed (i.e., thoughts of dying or distraction with physical pain can serve to avoid emotional pain). Thus, it is important to determine if these behaviors can be managed to proceed with the exposures to ultimately bring the client relief from a source of his or her distress. Peer consultation and/or consultation with an expert in trauma-focused PTSD treatment is recommended in these higher risk cases.

Underengagement and Related Reactions

Underengagement is another possibility when using behavioral interventions for PTSD. Underengagement occurs when a client fails or refuses to engage emotionally or focus on his or her distress during an exposure.

In these cases, the client may be doing the exposures but not showing any signs or showing only minimal signs of anxiety or distress. Failing to engage or focus on one's anxiety or distress during an exposure will likely prevent clients from benefiting from the exercise, because they do not experience the rise and fall of their anxiety and hence do not learn that they are capable of coping, nor do they gain new information about the feared stimuli.

Clients may underengage during exposures in a number of ways. They may use distraction to get through exposures. In these cases, they avert their focus, either overtly or covertly, and avoid directing their attention to the distressing stimulus and their anxiety. The therapist should strongly discourage this therapy-interfering behavior and supportively reiterate the rationale for avoiding it. Distraction should be conceptualized as a type of avoidance behavior that prevents new learning and maintains PTSD.

Signs that a client is underengaged in the imaginal exposure include his or her telling the story as if reading a police report, telling you about a movie he or she saw recently, or leaving out details of the traumatic experience. To address these issues, the therapist should remind the client to speak in the first person and use present tense, and to keep his or her eyes closed and try to visualize the event. In addition, well placed questions about the client's sensory experiences (e.g., What do you hear? What does it smell like?) may assist the client in engaging with the memory. When using this strategy, the therapist must balance helping the client engage with the memory against being overly distracting through the use of too many questions.

Similarly, a client may *white knuckle* his way through an exposure, not fully submitting himself to the emotional reactions and memories of the traumatic event. In this way, the client convinces himself to push through the distress with the idea that the exposure will soon be over. This can be likened to holding one's breath under water; the longer one holds his breath, the more distressing the experience becomes, until there is a sudden relief after resurfacing, or with exposures, when they conclude. We strongly discourage clients from approaching exposures in this manner, as this runs contrary to the purpose of immersing oneself in the exposure exercises. This strategy serves the same function as a distraction technique and prevents clients from focusing and fully engaging with the stimulus and their anxiety. Furthermore, it prevents clients from gaining new information about the feared stimulus and learning that they can cope with their anxiety.

Responding to the Client Who Wants to Stop

A client may ask to stop an exposure at any time during the exercise. We suggest being empathic by validating the distress that the client is experiencing while encouraging her or him to continue. In these cases, articulating the rationale for continuing the exposure is crucial (i.e., one does not want to sensitize the client to her or his anxiety to the memory or feared stimuli). However, it is ultimately the client's choice as to whether the exposure stops or not, and it is important to relay that the client is in control, and that you, as the therapist, will respect their decision. In general, strategies that may set up clients for success include a collaboratively planned exposure, ensuring the client is committed, and delivering a strong rationale prior to commencing the exercise.

Safety Concerns During In Vivo Exposures

A common feature of PTSD is overestimation of threat. Clients often overestimate the danger associated with a specific object or situation. In vivo exposures are designed to directly address the overestimation of threat and recalibrate one's ability to properly assess and interpret danger. Nevertheless, there will occasionally be scenarios in which a therapist must balance assigning an in vivo exposure with putting the client at real risk.

The overarching principle in assessing the objective safety of in vivo exposures is to consider whether the person would be in real danger if he or she had not experienced the traumatic event. For example, if a client was sexually assaulted in a parking lot, late at night, in a dangerous neighborhood where several other assaults have occurred, you may collaboratively make the decision that revisiting this particular parking lot is not in the best interest of the client. However, if the client has a fear or anxiety reaction when in all parking lots, regardless of their objective safety, exposure to different parking lots may be a good alternative.

Other scenarios in which exposures need to be balanced with safety are cases involving the confrontation of the perpetrator of the traumatic event (e.g., perpetrators of childhood sexual abuse, a sexual assault, or a physical assault). As a general rule, we do not recommend conducting an exposure that involves confrontation of the perpetrator, especially if there is any chance that the individual may continue to be a threat to the client (e.g., abusive partner). However, exposure to related stimuli currently causing distress or being avoided that do not pose an objective threat to the client may be ideal substitutes. For example, in the case of a sexual assault the client may conduct an exposure to reading a police report that includes details of the perpetrator. In the case of childhood sexual abuse by a male family member, exposure to other male members of the family may be ideal. Ensuring the safety of a client should always come before engaging in an exposure; however, anxiety or distress, in and of itself, is not dangerous. Although ensuring client safety can pose a challenge to conducting successful in vivo exposures, therapists must be creative and work around difficult scenarios in order to ensure that their clients maximally benefit from exposures.

Noncompliance With Homework

Regardless of the therapeutic intervention used, noncompliance with homework is a common occurrence that needs to be addressed. Specific to behavioral interventions for PTSD, exposure interventions rely heavily on repetition to ensure that habituation and new learning take place. As a result, homework completion is imperative in behavioral therapy. A primary reason that clients may not complete their homework is that they do not understand what they have been asked to do. Thus, ensuring that the client fully understands the assignment is crucial. After ensuring that the client understood the assigned homework and did not have a specific, acceptable reason for not completing it (e.g., sudden death of family member, medical hospitalization), we recommend highlighting the association between homework completion and treatment outcomes and noting the importance of repetition in exposure therapy as strategies to encourage completion of homework assignments.

If a client is not completing the majority of the assigned homework by the second or third session of therapy, we recommend having a detailed discussion about the barriers to homework completion. For example, a client may experience high levels of distress when completing homework and thus avoid the assignments. Clients may also indicate that they forget to complete the assignments given their busy schedules. In general, efforts to troubleshoot barriers to homework completion should be made. Making a specific plan to overcome these barriers is also helpful. This can include telephone calls or e-mails between sessions to remind and encouwwrage clients to complete their homework, or reinforcing the rationale associated with the homework assignments.

If homework noncompliance becomes a recurring issue and the strategies outlined above result in little change, having a candid discussion about the client's commitment to therapy may be helpful. This discussion should include issues such as whether this is the right time for him or her to engage in treatment, as well as whether the treatment plan is well-suited to his or her individual preferences.

CONCLUSION

With a number of studies supporting its efficacy, trauma-focused behavioral interventions for PTSD represent important therapeutic skills for clinicians treating this condition. Imaginal and in vivo exposures represent key behavioral strategies that may be used independently, as part of more general cognitive-behavioral therapy, or together as is done in the prolonged exposure protocol. These techniques aim to decrease avoidance and escape behaviors in order to increase habituation to the fear response and promote new learning. Through these techniques, clients are able to disprove their predictions about the threat or negative consequences associated with trauma-related cues and the memory of the traumatic event, as well as learn that their fear will reduce with repeated exposure to these triggers.

3

Trauma-Focused Interventions: Cognitive Techniques and Treatment Packages

As discussed in Chapter 1 regarding case conceptualization, cognitive theories of posttraumatic stress disorder (PTSD) hold that trauma survivors have maladaptive appraisals of traumatic experiences that remain unreconciled with prior positive beliefs about one's self, others, and the world, or seemingly serve to confirm prior negative beliefs in these areas. Distress surrounding trauma memories leads people to consciously avoid thinking about these memories, which results in poorly elaborated and contextualized trauma narratives. Trauma appraisals also have cascading effects on current negative interpretations about one's self, others, the world in general, and future events. Moreover, individuals with PTSD also have negative attentional biases toward perceived threat and negative events more generally, and they underestimate their ability to cope with future negative events, which serves to maintain PTSD

http://dx.doi.org/10.1037/14372-004
Treating PTSD With Cognitive-Behavioral Therapies: Interventions That Work, by C. M. Monson and P. Shnaider

symptomatology. Thus, the overarching goal of trauma-focused cognitive interventions for PTSD is to help trauma survivors systematically examine their trauma memories to further elaborate the context in which the trauma occurred and to reappraise specific traumatic events in a healthier way, in order to facilitate recovery. Trauma-focused cognitive therapies can also focus on here-and-now trauma-related cognitions that are conceptualized to emanate from traumatic experiences, but prioritize historical cognitions because of their hypothesized central role in the onset of PTSD symptoms.

In this chapter, we provide an overview of the most common strategies to induce trauma-specific cognitive change (i.e., Socratic dialogue, cognitive worksheets); we use a case example to illustrate these techniques. We then offer an overview of cognitive processing therapy (CPT; Resick, Monson, & Chard, 2008), the most-validated cognitively focused treatment package for PTSD and its comorbidities. Finally, we discuss common challenges in doing trauma-focused cognitive therapy for PTSD.

OVERVIEW OF KEY INTERVENTIONS

The overall goal of the cognitive interventions described below is to change thoughts and beliefs specifically related to traumatic experiences in order to induce emotional and behavioral changes. These interventions have generally been described elsewhere as *cognitive restructuring* techniques. Based on advances in neuroscience and basic learning research (e.g., Bouton, 2000, 2004; Craske et al., 2008), we believe it is most accurate to think about cognitive change as occurring because of the positive influence of more adaptive thoughts about events and not because the original thought itself is restructured or modified, and thereby no longer existent.

This conception has important implications for the delivery of cognitive interventions. More specifically, it argues for the need for repetition and practice to strengthen the neuronal pathways of new thoughts and connections to events in relation to old thoughts that are well-learned and rehearsed. Many clients resonate to the metaphor of the work involved in blazing a new path of thinking over a path that has been well traveled. Another implication is the importance of clinicians' validating clients' experiences of continuing to have old ways of thinking, and not urging them to avoid thinking the original thoughts through suppression or distraction. Years of cognitive psychology research have documented the paradoxical effect of telling people not to think of things or to suppress thoughts (for a review, see Wenzlaff & Wegner, 2000). Consequently, we encourage clinicians to simultaneously validate the presence of old thoughts while reinforcing the practice of alternative thoughts. A final implication of this conception of cognitive change is that a specific alternative thought counteracting the original thought may not be necessary. Rather, a range of alternatives may be more helpful in diluting the potency of the PTSD-related thought, which is also consistent with more recent writings about the role of cognitive flexibility in psychopathology (Deveney & Deldin, 2006; Tchanturia et al., 2004). Thus, we encourage clinicians to help their clients brainstorm a range of alternatives to the original thought in order to weaken the pathway to the original thought and develop the more adaptive cognitive connections associated with the traumatic event (for further discussion and a related cognitive intervention approach, see Monson & Fredman, 2012).

Socratic Dialogue

A cornerstone practice in most contemporary cognitive therapies for various mental health conditions is *Socratic questioning* or *Socratic dialogue*. Applied to trauma-focused cognitive interventions for PTSD, in this practice the clinician asks a series of questions that are designed to bring the client to a healthier appraisal of traumatic events. This practice is grounded in the Socratic method of learning, which values the power of individuals coming to know something new versus being given an insight or knowledge from another, as well as the benefits of modeling to clients a method of coming to know something (i.e., curiosity and inquisitiveness; Anderson & Goolishian, 1992; Padesky, 1993; Thase & Beck, 1993). Several clinicians and researchers (Bolten, 2001; Rutter, Friedberg, VandeCreek, & Jackson, 1999) have argued for the use of the term *Socratic dialogue* versus *Socratic questioning* to support the notion that the client and the clinician, in a psychotherapy context, are in a more equally balanced exchange with one another. This is in contrast to a power-imbalanced, teacher–student relationship in which the teacher is tasked with asking questions of the student who needs to learn prescribed knowledge. Engaged in Socratic dialogue, the clinician and client are joined as a team with the client bringing his or her life experiences, including traumatic experiences and interpretations of those experiences, and the clinician bringing his or her expertise to bear on trauma recovery and cognitive interventions.

Various writers have offered different classes of questions that might be posed when engaging in Socratic dialogue (e.g., Bishop & Fish, 1999; Elder & Paul, 1998; Paul & Elder, 2006; Wright, Basco, & Thase, 2006). We offer a synthesis of these prior efforts, offering a hierarchical approach to the types of questions that a cognitive therapist might pose when engaging in Socratic dialogue for trauma-related cognitions. Table 3.1 contains examples of questions at each level of the hierarchy, which are aimed at challenging common problematic thoughts found among individuals with PTSD.

Clarifying Questions

At the most foundational level, the therapist should be asking as many *clarifying questions* as possible to establish what was going on at the time of the traumatic event. It is extremely important for clinicians doing trauma-focused therapy to be willing to ask sensitive and difficult questions and to ask them as nonjudgmentally and matter-of-factly as possible. An example that comes from working with childhood and adult sexual assault/abuse survivors is the ability to inquire whether they experienced sexual arousal during an assault. The client may deduce that a sexual response during the event means that he wanted to be assaulted or was in some way responsible for his assault. Childhood sexual abuse survivors also commonly remark that there were pleasurable aspects of their assaults (e.g., feeling special to, emotionally intimate with, or cared about by the perpetrator). To engender recovery, it is important to ask these questions and discuss the answers as supportively as possible.

Challenging Assumptions

At the next level of depth are questions aimed at challenging assumptions that underlie clients' conclusions about traumatic events. Drawing from cognitive-behavioral conjoint therapy for PTSD (Monson & Fredman,

Table 3.1

Examples of Questions Used at Increasing Levels of Depth in Socratic Dialogue to Challenge Common Problematic Cognitions Associated With PTSD

Clarifying Questions	Who was there at the time?
	What did they do?
	What happened just before? Afterward?
	What were you thinking and feeling at the time?
	What was your state of mind (e.g., sleep-deprived, substance use)?
	What is protocol in these types of situations?
Challenging Assumptions	What other things could have happened had you done something differently?
	Have you ever met a good person who had bad things happen to them?
	What information did you have at the time of the event, not now that the event is over?
	What else could have happened had you fought back?
	Should one event define your entire character?
Evaluating Objective Evidence	What is the probability of _____ (safety concern) in your current circumstances?
	Do you know of at least one exception to your current conclusion?
	Can you think of at least one time when your expected outcome did not happen?
Challenging Underlying or Core Beliefs	What would it mean if you didn't blame yourself for what happened?
	What is there to like about this thought that is hard to change?
	If you changed this thought, how would you need to change your thoughts about yourself? Your thoughts about others?

2012), common misappraisals involve hindsight bias, just-world thinking, neglecting the situational context, trying to undo the traumatic event by imagining alternative behaviors and outcomes, and happily-ever-after thinking (i.e., assuming a different action would have resulted in a positive outcome). A common overarching assumption that individuals with PTSD have when appraising traumatic events is that they or someone else could have exerted more control over the traumatic event or its outcome.

This assumption is evidenced in clients' efforts to exert hindsight bias on the situation—"If I would have turned left instead of right," "If I would have fought back I wouldn't have been assaulted," or "I should have jumped into the water after him." Individuals with PTSD fail to appreciate that an alternative action may have had an equally negative or worse consequence.

Another assumption held by individuals with PTSD that should be challenged is the *just-world belief* (Lerner, 1980). The just-world belief holds that good things happen to good people, and bad things happen to bad people. Consistent with the above-described assumption about the ability to predict and control outcomes, this belief calls for an orderly, cause-and-effect association between an individual's behavior and consequences. In the case of traumatic events, which are construed as bad things, those with PTSD will assume that they did something bad to deserve them and will go about trying to find the prior bad behavior or bad behavior within the traumatic event that accounts for the bad outcome.

It is important that clinicians doing trauma-focused cognitive therapy do not make assumptions about the context surrounding traumatic events. We have observed therapists who assumed positive intentions on the part of their clients, leaving their clients reticent to describe actions, thoughts, or feelings about the traumatic event that they believe might be perceived as running contrary to the therapist's positive assumptions about the event. For example, one therapist assumed that his veteran client followed the rules of engagement as a combatant but later learned that his client had violated some of these rules. Later in therapy, the veteran expressed his self-recrimination, guilt, shame, and self-directed anger related to the event because the therapist had made assumptions about the client's role in the event. Conversely, we have observed therapists who made negative assumptions about their client, resulting in impeded therapy progress. For example, a clinician may make attributions about the blame that should be allocated to clients if the victim consumed substances prior to the traumatic event. Substance use may or may not play a role in traumatic events; it is only with careful consideration of the amount and context of substance use and the intentions of the client that the therapist and client can better assess the role of substances in the event, which ultimately facilitates processing of the traumatic event.

Evaluating Objective Evidence

Assuming there are no problematic assumptions underlying clients' conclusions, the next level of Socratic dialogue that we recommend is aimed at helping clients evaluate evidence that may or may not support the conclusions they have drawn. As mentioned previously, individuals with PTSD have a cognitive bias toward perceived threat and negative information. Thus, they will have this information more accessible to them and may overvalue it relative to data that do not necessarily support their conclusions. A client's overestimations of here-and-now danger is a common example of when a therapist might use Socratic dialogue focused on evaluating objective evidence for the PTSD-related thought. The overestimation of threat in situations such as being in a crowd, being in open spaces outside of combat or peacekeeping zones, driving motor vehicles, and seeing plastic bags on the side of the road (i.e., all potentially reminiscent of improvised explosive devices) are examples of situations that a trauma-focused cognitive therapist is likely to encourage clients to more objectively evaluate.

Challenging Underlying or Core Beliefs

Clients in cognitive therapy may report that they understand intellectually that their thinking does not make sense but do not appreciate it emotionally, or they may report that emotional changes are not occurring with their new thoughts. On these occasions we encourage trauma-focused cognitive therapists to consider the possibility that a client's deeper underlying belief may be preventing her or him from fully embracing an alternative way of thinking. Deeper beliefs often guard against the implications involved in changing one's thoughts. For example, if a trauma survivor truly believes the thought that she could not have done anything more to prevent the traumatic event from happening, this implies that she could be placed in a traumatic situation in the future in which she may or may not be able to change the outcome. In essence, changes in appraisals about traumatic events have cascading implications for here-and-now and future-oriented beliefs. In this case, the new appraisal is incongruent with the desire to retain the belief that the future is predictable and controllable. Another example is the case of an incest survivor who places more blame on himself than on his offending and nonoffending parents, because blaming them has deeper implications for his beliefs about his parents and his ongoing relationships with them, as well as his views on the responsibility of caregivers more generally.

Deeper cognitive intervention may also be necessary when individuals with PTSD have preexisting negative core beliefs or schemas. As discussed in Chapter 1, these preexisting beliefs may serve as a risk factor for the occurrence of PTSD upon exposure to a traumatic event. In these cases, the cognitive therapist would likely need to probe more deeply to determine how the client came to these beliefs prior to the trauma (e.g., aversive childhood experiences, invalidating environments), and work with the client to collaboratively challenge these deeper or core beliefs in order to prevent him or her from making trauma appraisals that seem to confirm the negative belief. For instance, if a client had a preexisting schema that he was worthless, he may be prone to thinking that he deserved the traumatic event and engage in self-blaming attributions. Changing self-blame appraisals about the trauma runs contrary to the deeper negative belief, often necessitating deeper cognitive intervention on this core schema to engender emotional and behavioral change.

Cognitive Worksheets

Beginning with Beck's (1979) seminal work on cognitive therapy for depression, a number of different types and formats of worksheets have been developed to assist clients in challenging their problematic thoughts. These worksheets have been labeled *Thought Records, Challenging Beliefs Worksheets, Five-Column Worksheets,* and so forth. (see Exhibit 3.1). Their purpose is to help clients distinguish thoughts from emotions and behaviors, challenge unhelpful thoughts, identify more adaptive alternative thoughts, and then consider the effects of the alternative thought(s) on their emotions and behavior. In using these worksheets, clients are generally taught

---

Exhibit 3.1

Challenging Questions Worksheet for Clients

Challenging Questions

Below is a list of questions to be used in helping you challenge your maladaptive or problematic thoughts. Not all questions will be appropriate for the thought you choose to challenge.

Thought: _____

1. What is the evidence for this thought?
2. What is the evidence against this thought?
3. Is your thought a habit or based on facts?
4. Are you thinking in all-or-none or exaggerated terms?
5. Are you thinking about all parts of the situation or only focusing on one aspect?
6. Does your information come from a reliable source?
7. Are you confusing a high probability with a low probability?
8. Are your judgments based on facts or feelings?
9. Are you focused on factors that really do not matter?

Note. From *Cognitive Processing Therapy: Veteran/Military Version,* by P. A. Resick, C. M. Monson, and K. M. Chard, 2008, Washington, DC: U.S. Department of Veterans Affairs. In the public domain.

---

common problematic thinking errors or cognitive distortions such as personalization, dichotomous thinking, mind-reading, over- and underestimating probabilities, and overgeneralizing (for further discussion on cognitive distortions and thinking errors, see Beck, 1979; Burns, 1999).

In trauma-focused cognitive therapy, the process of completing these worksheets is similar to that used for a range of disorders. Specific to trauma-focused cognitive therapy is the content of the thoughts and beliefs examined. We have identified four different classes of thoughts that are generally targeted in trauma-focused cognitive therapy: (a) thoughts about approaching trauma material, (b) thoughts about the trauma itself, (c) here-and-now thoughts that emanate from the trauma, and (d) thoughts about one's ability to cope with aversive or traumatic events in the future.

Thoughts About Approaching Trauma Material

Individuals with PTSD often have negative beliefs about what will happen if they think or talk about their trauma memories, as well as negative thoughts about the prognosis of their PTSD symptoms. This negative forecasting is an important cognitive target that may need to be addressed prior to conducting trauma-focused work, because it can often act as a barrier to engaging in trauma-focused interventions. It is also imperative to evaluate these beliefs if the client exhibits or expresses reluctance to engage in specific trauma-focused interventions. Remember that these cognitions are often based on irrelevant, mistaken, or missing data. For example, clients may have gotten inaccurate information on the treatability of PTSD from health care professionals, websites, or publications. Hence a cognitive therapist might encourage them to seek information from reputable sources about the prognosis of PTSD with evidence-based treatments and information about treatment options as part of their completion of a cognitive worksheet. Other clients may have, in the past, become overwhelmed when thinking about their traumatic event. For example, we had a client who had been psychiatrically hospitalized because of her trauma symptoms and was using this as evidence for the thought "I will become crazy again if I talk about my trauma." Using a cognitive worksheet she was able to arrive at the alternative thought "I wasn't choosing to look at my memories in treatment at the time. They were choosing to come to me. Maybe this isn't the best evidence to rely on for my belief that talking and thinking about the trauma would make me go crazy." As a result of the worksheet, her anxiety decreased to a more manageable level, and she was able to initiate trauma-focused cognitive therapy.

Another principle to consider in coaching clients in their use of worksheets for these types of thoughts is that they are forecasting an unknown future—and are likely forecasting only possible negative outcomes. To counter this tendency toward catastrophizing, clients can be coached to consider a range of possible outcomes, including neutral (e.g., "I might not get better or worse as a result of doing this therapy") and positive outcomes (e.g., "I might not have PTSD symptoms that impair my life if I do this therapy").

Thoughts About the Traumatic Event

Clients with PTSD often retrospect about the trauma and make appraisals that are designed to exert a sense of control or predictability about the occurrence of the event. In doing this, they often disregard or overlook important aspects of the trauma. In coaching clients to use cognitive worksheets for these thoughts, focus on the situational factors and information they had at the time of the event, and not what they know now months or years posttrauma. Therefore, a key problematic thinking error to be aware of is taking situations out of context. Contextualizing the trauma memory is an important ingredient to recovery from trauma from a cognitive perspective.

A common problematic trauma appraisal involves hindsight bias and the conclusion that alternative actions would have resulted in more positive outcomes. A childhood sexual abuse survivor we treated held the belief that if she would have told her mother, her sister's abuse could have been prevented. However, careful examination of the situational context of the client's abuse revealed that her uncle, the perpetrator, had insinuated that he would hurt her sister if the client were to tell anyone about the abuse. The client also reported that her mother and uncle were very close and she had not wanted to disrupt their relationship. The therapist worked with the client to help her appreciate the fact that she had actually been trying to protect her sister and her mother, given what she knew at the time. In addition, it is impossible to know whether the abuse would have stopped with disclosure and/or whether disclosure would have led her uncle to hurt her sister.

Here-and-Now Thoughts Emanating From the Traumatic Event

Individuals with PTSD have attentional biases toward perceived threat and negativity more generally when interpreting day-to-day experiences

(Ehlers & Clark, 2000). They tend to believe that certain people, places, and situations pose more risk than they objectively do. For example, a client who had been severely electrocuted became phobic of electrical outlets and switches, refusing to be near them. His hypervigilance included consistent monitoring of them when he was forced to go out, and he eventually moved to a cabin with minimal electricity to assuage his anxiety. His thoughts related to electricity involved overgeneralized and catastrophic risk. As a result of his trauma, he also had many thoughts that involved self-doubt in day-to-day decision making, because he believed that he should have done something else at the time of the electrocution to protect himself. Therefore, he had difficulty making decisions about current day events and often procrastinated or deferred decision-making to the few others in his life.

Because many traumas resulting in PTSD are interpersonal in nature (e.g., rape, physical assault), there also tend to be disruptions in trust, interpersonal control, and intimacy in later relationships (Freyd, 1996; McCann & Pearlman, 1990). Common thoughts include "If I get close to someone, they will hurt me," "Others cannot be trusted to protect me," and "People are unpredictable and dangerous." These thoughts often lead those with PTSD to avoid relationships or to distance themselves emotionally when they are in relationships.

The goal with these here-and-now thoughts are to arrive at more balanced and realistic appraisals of risk. All situations, places, and people are not safe and without risks. The goal is to help clients discern when there is objective risk versus perceived risk, when risk is objectively low. In other words, there are places and times to be vigilant; however, *hyper*vigilance can actually be detrimental to appreciating the places where and times when objective threats do exist.

Thoughts About One's Ability to Cope With Future Aversive or Traumatic Events

In addition to overestimating the likelihood of experiencing traumatic events, individuals with PTSD tend to underestimate their ability to cope with future negative or traumatic events (Ehlers & Clark, 2000). They often believe they will "go crazy," "lose it emotionally," or otherwise be unable to manage their emotional and physical reactions if reexposed to stressful events. The goal with these types of thoughts is to increase the client's sense of mastery and ability to cope if he or she is indeed reexposed. For example, a female sexual assault survivor was convinced she would have an emotional breakdown if she were to be assaulted again. As a result, she refused to be around men, let alone be in an intimate relationship with a man. In addition to addressing her overgeneralized beliefs related to the danger of *all* men, cognitive interventions were aimed at appreciating her ability to deal with her emotions and to take care of herself if another assault were to happen. This included a review of her ability to cope emotionally and physically in the aftermath of her prior sexual assault and in the face of other adversities that she had experienced. It also involved consideration of concrete behaviors that she could use to self-soothe and manage in the face of future stressful events in an effort to inoculate her against them.

Case Example: Jill

Jill, a 32-year-old Afghanistan war veteran, had been experiencing PTSD symptoms for over 5 years. She consistently avoided thoughts and images related to witnessing her fellow service members being hit by an improvised explosive device (IED) while driving a combat supply truck. Over the years, Jill became increasingly depressed and began using alcohol on a daily basis to help assuage her PTSD symptoms. She had difficulties in her employment, missing many days of work, and she reported feeling disconnected and numb around her husband and children. In addition to a range of other PTSD symptoms, Jill had a recurring nightmare of the event in which she was the leader of a convoy and her lead truck broke down. She waved the second truck forward, the truck that hit the IED, while she and her fellow service members on the first truck worked feverishly to repair it. Consistent with the traumatic event, her nightmare included images of her and the service members on the first truck smiling and waving at those on the second truck, and the service members on the second truck making fun of the broken truck and their efforts to fix it—"Look at that piece of junk truck—good luck getting that clunker fixed."

After a thorough assessment of her PTSD and comorbid symptoms, psychoeducation about PTSD symptoms, and a rationale for using trauma-focused cognitive interventions, Jill received 10 sessions of cognitive therapy for PTSD. She was first assigned cognitive worksheets to begin self-monitoring events, her thoughts about these events, and consequent feelings. These worksheets were used to sensitize Jill to the types of cognitions that she was having about current day events and to appraisals that she had about the explosion. For example, one of the thoughts she recorded related to the explosion was, "I should have had them wait and not had them go on." She recorded her related feeling to be guilt. Jill's therapist used this worksheet as a starting point for engaging in Socratic dialogue, as shown in the following example:

Therapist: Jill, do you mind if I ask you a few questions about this thought that you noticed, "I should have had them wait and not had them go on?"

Client: Sure.

Therapist: Can you tell me what the protocol tells you to do in a situation in which a truck breaks down during a convoy?

Client: You want to get the truck repaired as soon as possible, because the point of a convoy is to keep the trucks moving so that you aren't sitting ducks.

Therapist: The truck that broke down was the lead truck that you were on. What is the protocol in that case?

Client: The protocol says to wave the other trucks through and keep them moving so that you don't have multiple trucks just sitting there together more vulnerable.

Therapist: Okay. That's helpful for me to understand. In light of the protocol you just described and the reasons for it, why do you think you should have had the second truck wait and not had them go on?

Client: If I hadn't have waved them through and told them to carry on, this wouldn't have happened. It is my fault that they died. (Begins to cry)

Therapist: (Pause) It is certainly sad that they died. (Pause) However, I want us to think through the idea that you should have had them wait and not had them go on, and consequently that it was your fault. (Pause) If you think back about what you knew at the time—not what you know now 5 years after the outcome—did you see anything that looked like a possible explosive device when you were scanning the road as the original lead truck?

Client: No. Prior to the truck breaking down, there was nothing that we noticed. It was an area of Iraq that could be dangerous, but there hadn't been much insurgent activity in the days and weeks prior to it happening.

Therapist: Okay. So, prior to the explosion, you hadn't seen anything suspicious.

Client: No.

Therapist: When the second truck took over as the lead truck, what was their responsibility and what was your responsibility at that point?

Client: The next truck that Mike and my other friends were on essentially became the lead truck, and I was responsible for trying to get my truck moving again so that we weren't in danger.

Therapist: Okay. In that scenario then, would it be Mike and the others' jobs to be scanning the environment ahead for potential dangers?

Client: Yes, but I should have been able to see and warn them.

Therapist: Before we determine that, how far ahead of you were Mike and the others when the explosion occurred?

Client: Oh (pause), probably 200 yards?

Therapist: 200 yards—that's two football fields' worth of distance, right?

Client: Right.

Therapist: You'll have to educate me. Are there explosive devices that you wouldn't be able to detect 200 yards ahead?

Client: Absolutely.

Therapist: How about explosive devices that you might not see 10 yards ahead?

Client: Sure. If they are really good, you wouldn't see them at all.

Therapist: So, in light of the facts that you didn't see anything at the time when you waved them through at 200 yards behind and that they obviously didn't see anything 10 yards ahead before they hit the explosion, and that protocol would call for you preventing another danger of being sitting ducks, help me understand why you wouldn't have waved them through at that time? Again, based on what you knew at the time?

Client: (Quietly) I hadn't thought about the fact that Mike and the others obviously didn't see the device at 10 yards, as you say, or they would have probably done something else. (Pause) Also, when you say that we were trying to prevent another danger at the time of being "sitting ducks," it makes me feel better about waving them through.

Therapist: Can you describe the type of emotion you have when you say, "It makes me feel better?"

Client: I guess I feel less guilty.

Therapist: That makes sense to me. As we go back and more accurately see the reality of what was really going on at the time of this explosion, it is important to notice that it makes you feel better emotionally. (Pause) In fact, I was wondering if you had ever considered that, in this situation, you actually did exactly what you were supposed to do and that something worse could have happened had you chosen to make them wait?

Client: No. I haven't thought about that.

Therapist: Obviously this was an area that insurgents were active in if they were planting explosives. Is it possible that it could have gone down worse had you chosen not to follow protocol and send them through?

Client: Hmmm. I hadn't thought about that either.

Therapist: That's okay. Many people don't think through what could have happened if they had chosen an alternative course of action at the time or they assume that there would have only been positive outcomes if they had done something different. I call it "happily ever after" thinking—assuming that a different action would have resulted in a positive outcome. (Pause) When you think, "I did a good job following protocol in a stressful situation that may have prevented more harm from happening," how does that make you feel?

Client: It definitely makes me feel less guilty.

Therapist: I'm wondering if there is any pride that you might feel?

Client: Hmmm . . . I don't know if I can go that far.

Therapist: What do you mean?

Client: It seems wrong to feel pride when my friends died.

Therapist: Is it possible to feel both pride and sadness in this situation? (Pause) Do you think Mike would hold it against you for feeling pride, as well as sadness for his and others' losses?

Client: Mike wouldn't hold it against me. In fact, he'd probably reassure me that I did a good job.

Therapist: (Pause) That seems really important for you to remember. It may be helpful to remind yourself of what you have discovered today, because you have some habits in thinking about this event in a particular way. We are also going to be doing some practice assignments [Challenging Questions Worksheets] that will help to walk you through your thoughts about what happened during this event, help you to remember what you knew at the time, and remind you how different thoughts can result in different feelings about what happened.

Client: I actually feel a bit better after this conversation.

Another thought that Jill described in relation to the traumatic event was, "I should have seen the explosion was going to happen to prevent my friends from dying." Her related feelings were guilt and self-directed anger. The therapist used this thought to introduce the cognitive intervention titled a *Challenging Thoughts Worksheet* (see Exhibit 3.2). The therapist first provided education about the different types of thinking errors, including habitual thinking, all-or-none thinking, taking things out of context, overestimating probabilities, and emotional reasoning, as well as discussed other important factors, such as gathering evidence for and

Exhibit 3.2

Challenging Thoughts Worksheet

A. Situation	B. Thought(s)	C. Emotion(s)	D. Challenging Thoughts	E. Alternative Thought(s)	F. Re-rate Old Thought(s)	G. Emotion(s)
Describe the event, thought or belief leading to the unpleasant emotion(s).	Write thought(s) related to Column A. Rate belief in each thought below from 0–100% (How much do you believe this thought?)	Specify sad, angry, etc., and rate how strongly you feel each emotion from 0–100%	Use **Challenging Questions** to examine your automatic thoughts from Column B. Is the thought balanced and factual or extreme?	What else can I say instead of Column B? How else can I interpret the event instead of Column B? Rate belief in alternative thought(s) from 0–100%	Re-rate how much you now believe the thought(s) in Column B from 0–100%	Now what do you feel? 0–100%
My fellow service members died in an explosion.	*"I should have seen the explosive device to prevent my friends from dying."* (100%) *Guilt (100%)* *Anger at self (75%)*		Evidence for? *I may have been able to see it.* Evidence against? *The point of these devices is for it to be well concealed.* Habit or fact? *It is a habit for me to blame myself for bad things happening.* All or none/exaggerated? *I'm "shoulding" on myself.* Focused on only one aspect? *I'm forgetting that they were on watch too.* Source unreliable? *I'm the source and others don't blame me.* High versus low probability? N/A Based on facts or feelings? *Feelings. Guilt = bad behavior.* Factors that matter? N/A	*"The best explosive devices aren't seen and Mike (driver of the second truck) was a good soldier. If he saw something he would have stopped or tried to evade it."* (90%)	10%	*Guilt (10%)* *Anger at self (5%)*

against the thought, evaluating the source of the information, and focusing on irrelevant factors. More specifically, Jill noted that she experienced 100% intensity of guilt and 75% intensity of anger at herself in relation to the thought "I should have seen the explosive device to prevent my friends from dying." She challenged this thought with several Challenging Questions, including the notion that improvised explosive devices are meant to be concealed, that she is the source of the information (because others don't blame her), and that her feelings are not based on facts (i.e., she feels guilt and therefore must be guilty). She came up with the alternative thought, "The best explosive devices aren't seen and Mike (driver of the second truck) was a good soldier. If he saw something he would stopped or tried to evade it," which she rated as 90% confidence in believing. She consequently believed her original thought 10%, and re-rated her emotions as only 10% guilt and 5% anger at self.

TRAUMA-FOCUSED COGNITIVE TREATMENT PACKAGE FOR PTSD: COGNITIVE PROCESSING THERAPY

One treatment package that consists predominantly of trauma-focused cognitive interventions, and is recommended as a first-line therapy in various treatment guidelines, is CPT (Resick, Monson, & Chard, 2008; see Table 3.2). The 12-session CPT protocol is described in a therapist manual; there is also a client workbook that includes out-of-session assignments. One advantage of CPT compared with other trauma-focused treatments is that it can be delivered in a group format.

CPT uses the cognitive intervention strategies described above to help clients arrive at healthier meanings about historical traumatic events, as well as current day and future anticipated events. Specific appraisals and attributions about traumatic events, and then more broad overgeneralized beliefs about oneself, others, and the world impacted by the trauma, are examined. Socratic dialogue and daily cognitive worksheet techniques are used to help clients identify and modify their distorted and maladaptive cognitions.

Table 3.2

Session-by-Session Guide to Cognitive Processing Therapy

Session	Key interventions	Homework
1	Psychoeducation about dynamic nature of PTSD symptoms Cognitive rationale for interventions, including notion of *stuck points* to recovery Anticipating and overcoming avoidance	Review handout regarding dynamic nature of PTSD symptoms Review handout regarding *stuck points* Write Impact Statement regarding beliefs about why the traumatic event occurred and the consequences of the appraisal on here-and-now thinking
2	Out-of-session assignment review Introduction of self-monitoring of the connection between events, thoughts, and emotions	Daily monitoring of events, thoughts, and emotions, of which at least one must be trauma-related
3	Out-of-session assignment review Initiate Socratic Dialogue regarding problematic trauma appraisals	Daily monitoring of events, thoughts, and emotions, of which at least one must be trauma-related Written trauma account and daily reading (if doing CPT version with written account)
4–5	Out-of-session assignment review Client reads written account aloud Therapist encourages natural emotions Therapist leads in Socratic Dialogue regarding problematic trauma appraisals	Daily monitoring of events, thoughts, and emotions, of which at least one must be trauma-related Written trauma account and daily reading (if doing CPT version with written account) In Session 5 teach Challenging Questions Worksheet to challenge single problematic belief
6–7	Out-of-session assignment review Client taught series of worksheets to challenge beliefs about the traumatic event or that emanate from the traumatic event	In Session 6 teach Patterns of Problematic Thinking to challenge patterns of problematic thinking In Session 7 teach Challenging Beliefs Worksheet

Table 3.2

Session-by-Session Guide to Cognitive
Processing Therapy (*Continued*)

Session	Key Interventions	Homework
8–11	Out-of-session assignment review Client uses Challenging Beliefs Worksheet to continue to challenge problematic trauma appraisals as well as beliefs about one's self and others that may be disrupted by trauma (i.e., safety, trust, power/control, esteem, intimacy)	Challenging Beliefs Worksheets on trauma appraisals and consequent beliefs In Session 10 assign behavioral assignments of noticing and giving compliments to others and doing non-contingent, self-nurturing behavior In Session 11 complete post-treatment Impact Statement regarding beliefs about why the traumatic event occurred and the consequences of the appraisal on here-and-now thinking
12	Out-of-session assignment review Review course of therapy Consolidation of treatment gains Planning for the future	Recommended follow-up appointment in approximately 3 months to monitor maintenance of gains and possible need for further treatment

Note. Data from Resick, Monson, and Chard (2008).

The protocol is divided into three phases: education, trauma processing, and teaching the client to challenge his or her own cognitions. In the first phase, the focus is on educating clients about the dynamic nature of PTSD symptoms, the cognitive rationale for the treatment interventions, and the connection between thoughts and feelings. In the second phase, the therapist and client work together to identify where the client has become *stuck* in his or her recovery from the traumatic event. Writing and reading narratives about the traumatic event can be used as a way of identifying these stuck points, though a version of the therapy that excludes the written trauma accounts (CPT-Cognitive Only [CPT-C]) has been shown to be efficacious and may actually lead to faster improvements across sessions (Resick, Galovski, et al., 2008). In the final phase, thoughts emanating from the trauma are examined, and collaboratively, new, more balanced beliefs about what the trauma means about oneself, others, and the world, are developed.

The research and clinical literature on CPT and CPT-C has consistently shown the therapy to be efficacious in reducing PTSD and other comorbid symptoms in the short and long term (i.e., 5+ years) in a range of traumatized samples (e.g., Chard, 2005; Forbes et al., 2012; Monson et al., 2006; Resick, Galovski, et al., 2008; Resick, Nishith, Weaver, Astin, & Feuer, 2002; Resick, Williams, Suvak, Monson, & Gradus, 2012; Surís, Link-Malcolm, Chard, Ahn, & North, 2013). A recent study tested a variable length application of the therapy (Galovski, Blain, Mott, Elwood, & Houle, 2012). In this study, participants received as few as four or as many as 18 sessions of CPT, depending on the client meeting specific end-state criteria assessed at each session: self-reported PTSD and depressive symptom scores below clinical cutoffs, agreement between the therapist and client that treatment goals have been attained, and independent assessment and confirmation, by a blinded assessor using a clinician-administered PTSD symptom interview, that the client no longer meets the diagnostic status for PTSD. More than half of the participants reached the end-state criteria prior to the 12th session, and an additional one third of participants were able to achieve the end-state criteria with additional CPT sessions. This study argues for dosing the number of CPT sessions based on an individual client's response to treatment versus uniform application of the 12-session protocol, and for continuing to provide additional sessions in those cases in which clients have not fully responded within 12 sessions of therapy.

COMMON CHALLENGES IN DOING TRAUMA-FOCUSED COGNITIVE INTERVENTIONS

Clinicians and clients face several common challenges in doing trauma-focused cognitive interventions for PTSD. These include clients not understanding the cognitive interventions, or feeling overwhelmed by them, being reluctant to consider alternative thoughts, and alternative thoughts not translating into emotional and behavioral change. Common challenges for clinicians include comfort and proficiency with using Socratic dialogue to help clients generate alternative thoughts and juggling clients' here-and-now concerns with the necessary targeted focus on trauma-related cognitions.

Common Client Challenges

One of the most common concerns related to trauma-focused cognitive interventions for PTSD is that the cognitive constructs will be too intellectually demanding or confusing for their clients. Clinicians often cite concerns that the cognitive worksheets will be too reminiscent of failed school experiences and too cognitively sophisticated for their clients. In our experience, these concerns are generally unfounded and can be addressed with the delivery of a strong rationale and by taking into account the intellectual and literacy abilities of their clients when delivering these interventions. For instance, CPT has been delivered to clients with overall intellectual quotients as low as 70 and literacy abilities as low as third grade (Nixon, Nishith, & Resick, 2004; Schulz, Resick, Huber, & Griffin, 2006). In those cases in which there are intellectual or literacy concerns, clinicians should adjust delivery of the interventions to use the simplest worksheets and language that is commensurate with the client's level of functioning. It is our experience that clients with high levels of intellect and cognitive abilities can actually be more difficult to treat because of their tendency toward intellectualization. Our clinical experience, as well as some data (Ehlers, Clark, Hackmann, McManus, & Fennell, 2005), indicates that those individuals with low educational attainment and a more concrete thinking style can be more amenable to cognitive interventions.

Other client challenges are reluctance to consider alternative thoughts or defensiveness surrounding original interpretations of traumatic events or current day events. Clients can be reluctant to change their minds for a variety of reasons, including the notion that changing their mind about interpretations means that they were wrong in thinking the original thoughts, guarding against a more threatening thought that would be the consequence of changing their thoughts, or believing that changing their thoughts would mean that the clinician somehow "won." When clients are reluctant to change their thoughts or resistant to other possible interpretations, it is imperative that clinicians not fight the resistance but back off to decrease it and maintain a good working alliance. These are opportunities for the clinician to assess whether she or he is engaging in effective Socratic dialogue and for helping the client with worksheets in a spirit of collaboration and curiosity.

If clients are able to generate alternatives but reluctant to accept a different, healthier perspective, clinicians might carefully pose questions aimed at the deeper implications of changing their mind, because, as discussed above, there are often deeper, more threatening cognitions that would result. Clinicians must be very careful in how they pose these questions if clients are already reluctant or resistant. Careful word choice and an empathic and curious delivery are crucial. For instance, the clinician might say, "I wonder if we can think about what it might mean if you believed your alternative thought in this case?"

It is common for clients receiving cognitive therapy to state that they intellectually understand or believe an alternative thought but that it does not lead to changed feelings or behaviors (e.g., "I know that the alternative is true, but I just don't feel it in my gut"). Clinicians should validate their clients for being able to intellectually consider an alternative, which is more than half the battle to change. There is a relative minority of cases in which clients have new insights that immediately translate into emotional change because they had not considered alternative cognitions. However, most change in cognitive therapy occurs through rehearsal and repetition of new alternative thoughts. Thus, clinicians should point this out to clients to instill and maintain hopefulness for change, and they should brainstorm with clients strategies to induce conscious attention to, and rehearsal of, new thoughts. Examples of these strategies include daily reading of successfully completed cognitive worksheets, paper notes with the alternative thoughts written on them for clients to carry with them in their pocket or wallet, computer screen savers with the alternative thoughts, scheduling electronic reminders in a calendar, or enlisting trusted others to remind the client of alternative, more adaptive thoughts.

Common Clinician Concerns

One of the common concerns that we hear from clinicians is that they do not feel adequately trained or comfortable in conducting Socratic dialogue. Clinicians are almost universally trained to paraphrase and reflect their clients' thoughts and feelings as part of their education in the non-specific but essential ingredients of any efficacious psychotherapy. Irrespective of the psychotherapy model practiced, clinicians also tend to be trained to offer their clients interpretations or directed guidance to solve presenting problems. Socratic dialogue includes paraphrasing and reflecting clients' thoughts and feelings, but it also involves the clinician asking questions aimed at bringing clients to a new way of construing traumatic events, as well as current and future events. In this way, we think it is better to consider Socratic dialogue a therapeutic stance or way of being in the therapeutic relationship versus a set of technical skills or questions that the clinician delivers. Like the development of any new skill, it takes consistent practice. However, this skill is highly generalizable to the treatment of a range of mental health conditions and a powerful tool in collaboratively working with clients to discover new and healthier ways of thinking. There are several texts and training videos available for more in-depth training in Socratic dialogue (Padesky, 1996; Wright et al., 2006).

Clinicians may also find themselves struggling to find the right balance in juggling clients' here-and-now life concerns with the targeted focus on historical trauma-related cognitions. We recommend that clinicians address here-and-now concerns using the cognitive skills they are seeking to teach the client. For example, they should encourage clients to use the cognitive worksheets on daily events to foster their development of the cognitive skills. This should help in generalizing and consolidating the skills beyond the focus on historical events. However, clinicians should be careful not to allow a focus on current life events to serve an avoidance function in the treatment of PTSD. It is our experience that if you are going to err on one side or another of the balance between a focus on historical or current events, it is better to focus more on trauma appraisals and creating a healthier narrative about the traumatic event rather than here-and-now thoughts that emanate from, or are a consequence of, the traumatic event. The rationale for this is that changing trauma-related cognitions will have downstream effects on current appraisals and attributions and clients' symptomatology and general functioning.

DIVERSITY ISSUES IN THE DELIVERY OF TRAUMA-FOCUSED COGNITIVE INTERVENTIONS FOR PTSD

Issues related to diversity—religion, culture, gender, sexuality—are inevitably raised when doing trauma-focused cognitive interventions. This is because traumatic experiences can run in opposition to, or need to be integrated into, one's religious or cultural beliefs. Depending on the nature of the traumatic event, questions about one's sexual orientation or negative views toward the opposite sex can be evoked.

Because traumatic events are, by definition, sentinel events in people's lives, some of the most basic existential issues come to the forefront, and people often turn to their religious or spiritual belief systems to make sense of these experiences. The ways in which religion and spirituality may surface in trauma-focused cognitive therapy for PTSD are highly dependent on the client's particular belief system and level of religious or spiritual orthodoxy. For example, one of us had a client who believed that she had been sexually assaulted as punishment from God because of having had premarital intercourse. Another client struggled because he believed that God had abandoned him in not saving his daughter from drowning.

Clinicians doing trauma-focused cognitive therapy need to be comfortable with asking their clients about their religious or spiritual beliefs, and they may need to encourage clients to sufficiently diversify their belief system to reconcile the traumatic event. It is crucial that the clinician adopt a curious and nonjudgmental approach when inquiring about the client's beliefs in this area, not imposing his or her own values or trying to talk the client out of the belief system. The goal is to find alternatives to the interpretations based on a given set of beliefs, or to develop a more nuanced set of beliefs based on experience and religious or spiritual teachings. Religious texts, for example, include stories about a higher power acting seemingly malevolent for a greater purpose or religious leaders suffering for a longer term outcome. In this vein, it may be helpful to have clients find such examples within their religious teachings. Enlisting the help of a trusted member of the clergy in those cases in which religious beliefs play a pivotal role in the interpretations of the trauma is also recommended. Clinicians do not have to be experts in various religions, but they must be willing to explore and discover their clients' specific religious beliefs and how those beliefs may be negatively affecting their trauma appraisals.

Likewise, cultural beliefs may influence trauma appraisals in the aftermath of traumatization. An example of this comes from some cultural beliefs about women's sexual victimization, including the notion that women are to blame for their sexual assaults and are undesirable as wives and mothers if they have been sexually assaulted. Similarly, some cultures may discount the possibility that men can be sexually victimized. In these cases it is important to work with the client to determine his or her own views on the acceptability of these notions, and perhaps having him or her discover that not all cultures subscribe to these views on sexual victimization.

Conversely, the ethnicity and cultural background of individuals involved in or the perpetrators of a trauma can lead to negative, overgeneralized beliefs about members of that ethnic or cultural group. For example, Vietnam and Iraq veterans with PTSD may have negative, stereotyped views about Vietnamese and Iraqi people, respectively. Similarly, victims of interpersonal traumas may develop negative views about individuals of a particular ethnicity based on the ethnicity of the perpetrator. These overgeneralized beliefs should be the target of intervention in trauma-focused cognitive therapy to alleviate the client's anxiety and/or anger related to individuals of different races and ethnicities.

It is common for men who were sexually victimized by other men to question their sexual identity, especially if they were sexually aroused at the time of the trauma. Providing psychoeducation about the automaticity of sexual arousal and the frequency of its occurrence in the context of sexual victimization (whether a male or female victim) is key to normalizing such experiences, which can be great sources of shame. Sexual arousal during a sexual assault can also lead to trying to make sense of things after the fact—"Did I really want to be sexually assaulted, given that I was aroused?" We have had success in using the analogy of tickling to educate about sexual arousal. It is very difficult to shut down the physical response to tickling, whether one wants to be tickled or not. Sexual arousal is similar; sexual arousal can even have a protective function of providing lubrication for women who experience penetrative sexual assault experiences.

Depending on the sex of the perpetrator of interpersonal trauma, individuals with PTSD can develop negative overgeneralized beliefs about the safety, trustworthiness, and overall value of the other sex. For example, a woman sexually assaulted by a man may conclude that all men are dangerous, only interested in having forced sex, and out to exploit women. Traumatic experiences can also serve to seemingly reinforce preexisting negative beliefs about the other sex. An example of this comes from a case of a male motor vehicle accident survivor who was hit by a car driven by a woman. This patient commented, "This is just further proof that women are bad drivers."

Trauma and its aftermath can also call into question one's gender identity. A man who is traumatized and has PTSD may question his masculinity, assuming that a "real man" could have prevented the traumatic event from happening or would not have mental health problems as a result. We have found this type of thinking to be relatively more common within the active duty and veteran populations where there is an emphasis on masculine ideals of strength, power, and invulnerability. Meanwhile, a woman who is sexually traumatized may question her femininity and desirability by men. Female sexual assault survivors often describe feeling dirty as a result of their sexual victimization, leaving them feeling less attractive and appealing.

CONCLUSION

A number of studies support the efficacy of trauma-focused cognitive interventions for PTSD and its common comorbidities. Socratic dialogue and cognitive worksheets designed to help clients challenge their maladaptive thoughts are key cognitive intervention strategies that have been found to be efficacious in cognitive-behavioral treatment packages for PTSD. These interventions serve to decrease avoidance of trauma memories by approaching them in a systematic manner, facilitate contextualization of the memories, and create more adaptive appraisals about the trauma. The interventions are also used to address here-and-now cognitions that are a consequence of the trauma and are conceptualized to maintain PTSD and other trauma-related sequelae.

4

Theory Underlying
Skills-Focused Interventions

Interventions have been developed and tested for posttraumatic stress disorder (PTSD) that do not entail the client revisiting the trauma memory. Rather, their foci are on managing the symptoms of the disorder or skills deficits associated with PTSD (e.g., stress management, interpersonal skills). Several different treatments have been developed in this class to manage PTSD symptoms and/or its common comorbidities (e.g., Najavits, 2002; Novaco, 1983).

In this chapter, we briefly describe the rationale and theoretical underpinnings for using these skills-focused interventions, specifically as they pertain to those interventions in this class that have the most empirical support, stress-inoculation training (SIT; Meichenbaum, 1985) and skills training in affective and interpersonal regulation (STAIR; Cloitre, Cohen, & Koenen, 2006).

http://dx.doi.org/10.1037/14372-005
Treating PTSD With Cognitive-Behavioral Therapies: Interventions That Work, by C. M. Monson and P. Shnaider

THEORY UNDERLYING
STRESS-INOCULATION TRAINING

A central concept underlying SIT is that of inoculation, which has been used in both medicine and social psychological research on attitude change. In medicine, vaccinations often involve exposure to weaker forms of a disease in order to ward off more severe reactions (e.g., smallpox vaccinations). Earlier exposure to a more moderate form of stress or disease serves to guard against reactions to future exposure because the initial exposure produces antibodies and physically prepares the body for a future attack.

In a parallel vein, McGuire (1964) observed that prior exposure to attitudinal information has a protective or *inoculating* effect against subsequent, more intense efforts at persuasion. The prior exposure to persuasive efforts seems to mobilize counterattitudinal strategies that can be used against subsequent conversion efforts. In both medical and attitudinal inoculation cases, a person's resistance is postulated to be enhanced by exposure to a stimulus strong enough to arouse defenses and coping processes without being so powerful that it debilitates the individual. Thus, SIT is based on the notion that exposing clients to graded forms of stress can bolster both coping mechanisms and confidence in using their coping repertoire.

Borrowing from Lazarus and Folkman's (1984) model, SIT adopts a transactional view of stress and coping that holds that stress occurs when the perceived demands of a situation exceed the perceived resources of the system to meet those demands. This view of stress emphasizes the critical role of cognitive-affective appraisal processes and coping activities. According to this transactional perspective, stress is neither a characteristic of the environment alone nor a characteristic of the person alone. In contrast, stress is defined as a bidirectional, dynamic relationship between the person and the environment.

Additionally, the constructive narrative perspective was drawn upon in the development of SIT, which holds that individuals construct narratives about themselves, others, the world, and the future. The nature and content of these narratives play critical roles in influencing coping processes. According to Meichenbaum and Fitzpatrick (1993), the narratives are organized around identifiable episodes, including intelligible plots and characters; they also convey goals and themes. Traumatic events are perceived to be defining moments in an individual's life story or narrative, and the narrative formed about the traumatic event influences emotional and behavioral coping. Maladaptive narratives outlined by Meichenbaum (2007) include self-focused cognitions that have a *victim* theme, such as seeing oneself as continually vulnerable and mentally defeated, dwelling on negative implications, being preoccupied with others' views, and imagining and ruminating about what might have happened in the traumatic event. They also include beliefs that changes posttrauma are permanent; that the world is unsafe, unpredictable, and untrustworthy; that the future will be negative; and that life has lost its meaning. In addition, they include cognitions related to blaming oneself and others, as well as comparisons between oneself and others, before versus after the trauma, and the current circumstance with what might have been.

THEORY UNDERLYING SKILLS TRAINING IN AFFECTIVE AND INTERPERSONAL REGULATION

There is substantial evidence that men and women with PTSD experience difficulties in regulating a range of emotions (e.g., Briere, 1988; Chemtob, Novaco, Hamada, Gross, & Smith, 1997; Monson, Price, Rodriguez, Ripley, & Warner, 2004). In addition, interpersonal relationship functioning, including intimate relationship discord and dissolution, social withdrawal and isolation, and poor social adjustment, are extremely common (Schnurr, Lunney, & Sengupta, 2004; Taft, Watkins, Stafford, Street, & Monson, 2011; Whisman, 1999). In fact, interpersonal problems have been found to be the most frequent precipitant for treatment in those with PTSD (Cloitre et al., 2006). Underscoring the importance of affective and interpersonal problems in those with PTSD, Cloitre, Miranda, Stovall-McClough, and Han (2005) found that, among women with a history of childhood abuse, emotion regulation and interpersonal problems predicted functional impairments above and beyond PTSD symptom severity. Thus, cognitive-behavioral interventions have been developed to specifically address these problems associated with PTSD.

STAIR is the treatment package for these problems that has the best empirical support. It is grounded in cognitive-behavioral and dialectical behavior theory indicating that individuals with PTSD do not have adequate skills to cope with emotion dysregulation, and they do not have interpersonal skills to successfully develop and maintain a range of interpersonal relationships. These skill deficits may be risk factors for PTSD in that individuals experiencing high levels of emotional distress after traumatization may engage in avoidant emotional coping (e.g., distraction, suppression) that ultimately impedes natural recovery. Similarly, those with poor interpersonal skills may be less likely to have adequate social support or the ability to solicit such support posttrauma. Alternatively, the onset of PTSD symptoms and its common comorbidities may impair emotional and interpersonal functioning skills. Regardless of the directionality of the symptoms and skill deficits, skill development is postulated to help manage the symptoms of PTSD and improve emotional and social functioning within this approach.

STAIR was originally conceived to be used as the first stage in a stage-based treatment model for survivors of childhood abuse, in which STAIR is followed by a modified version of prolonged exposure (Foa, Hembree, & Rothbaum, 2007) called *narrative therapy*. STAIR focuses on improving particular emotion regulation and interpersonal skills deficits theorized to be relevant to PTSD. Emotion regulation deficits outlined by the developers of STAIR include emotional reactivity (fear, rage, avoidance) to minor stimuli, difficulty in getting back to baseline or restoring a sense of emotional equilibrium, tendency to dissociate under stressful circumstances, engaging in self-injurious behaviors (e.g., self-cutting, burning), and coping via excessive alcohol or drug use (Cloitre, Stovall-McClough, Zorbas, & Charuvastra, 2008).

Problems with interpersonal skills outlined by the developers include difficulty with intimacy and trust, sensitivity to criticism, inability to hear other viewpoints, difficulty in standing up for oneself, tendency to quit jobs and relationships without negotiation, and a history of repeated victimization (Cloitre et al., 2008). The theory underlying STAIR also includes consideration of maladaptive interpersonal schemas, or cognitive-affective structures that organize information according to experience and then guide interpretation of future events (Safran & Segal, 1990). This cognitively oriented theory intersects with attachment theory (Bowlby, 1969/1982), and specifically the biologically based propensity to maintain closeness to available caretakers that functions to maximize survival. These interpersonal schemas are theorized to be influenced by early life attachment experiences with caregivers and can be negatively affected by disturbances in caretaking relationships, including trauma. Schemas are shaped by experience and also serve as templates that guide future expectations and behaviors. On the basis of their experiences, individuals with PTSD are theorized to have negative schemas about themselves and others, which can have a self-fulfilling nature in interpreting social circumstances.

CONCLUSION

PTSD is associated with a range of skills deficits that may be risk factors or consequences of the disorder. Clinicians can focus on improving these skills in order to facilitate clients' management of PTSD symptoms. The skills deficits that have been associated with, or are a product of, PTSD include poor stress management, emotion dysregulation, and difficulties in interpersonal relations. A better understanding of the specific nature of these skills deficits for a given client with PTSD can inform case conceptualization and thereby the treatment of these skills deficits to manage PTSD symptoms.

5

Skills-Focused Cognitive and Behavioral Interventions

As discussed in Chapter 4 of this volume, cognitive and behavioral theories underlying skills-focused interventions posit that post-traumatic stress disorder (PTSD) is a consequence or product of skills deficits, specifically in anxiety management, emotion regulation, and interpersonal functioning. Consequently, to manage the symptoms of PTSD and its common comorbidities or associated features, there have been interventions developed to address these problems. In this chapter, we review two empirically supported treatment packages that have been developed to address these symptoms or presenting problems: stress-inoculation training (SIT; Meichenbaum, 1985) and skills training in affective and interpersonal regulation (STAIR; Cloitre, Cohen, & Koenen, 2006).

http://dx.doi.org/10.1037/14372-006
Treating PTSD With Cognitive-Behavioral Therapies: Interventions That Work, by C. M. Monson and P. Shnaider

STRESS-INOCULATION TRAINING

Originally developed to treat a broad range of individuals with various stress-related conditions and presenting problems (e.g., panic disorder, anger control issues; Meichenbaum, 1985), SIT has since been specifically applied to the treatment of PTSD. Two randomized controlled trials including women with sexual assault–related PTSD tested the efficacy of SIT in treating PTSD (Foa et al., 1999; Foa, Rothbaum, Riggs, & Murdock, 1991). In Foa and colleagues' trials testing SIT, they purposefully removed in vivo exposure interventions contained within the original SIT protocol in order to not have overlapping interventions between prolonged exposure (PE) and SIT treatments. Even with this modification to SIT, their first trial found that SIT produced significantly more improvement in PTSD symptoms than did the supportive counseling (SC) and wait-list conditions immediately following treatment; PE outcomes were not significantly different from those of the other conditions at posttreatment. At 3-month follow-up including analysis of treatment completers only and comparison of the three active treatments (i.e., SIT, PE, SC), PE evidenced a marginally significant improvement in PTSD symptoms from posttreatment to follow-up. There were no changes in PTSD symptoms between posttreatment and follow-up for SIT or SC (Foa et al., 1991). In a follow-up study comparing PE, SIT, and their combination (PE/SIT), all three treatments led to improvements in PTSD, but there were no differences in symptom severity between the three conditions at posttreatment or at any of the follow-up assessments. PE produced superior improvements in general anxiety and global social adjustment at follow-up compared with the other two treatments (Foa et al., 1999).

SIT is designed to be flexibly delivered over eight to 14 sessions (i.e., it is not a prescribed session-by-session protocol) and can been administered in both individual and group formats. The treatment is designed to provide clients with a sense of mastery over their stress by teaching a variety of coping skills and then providing opportunities to practice those skills in a graduated or *inoculating* fashion. There are three phases of SIT (see Table 5.1).

Table 5.1

Phases of Stress-Inoculation Training

Phase	Title
1	**Conceptualization**

Identify determinants of the presenting problem.

Solicit narrative accounts of stress and coping to collaboratively identify a client's coping strengths/resources.

Disaggregate global stressors into specific stressful situations and break down stressful situations and reactions into specific behaviorally prescriptive problems.

Identify changeable and unchangeable aspects of stressful situations.

Establish short-term, intermediate, and long-term behaviorally specified goals.

Client self-monitoring of stressful situations and the role of stress-engendering appraisals, internal dialogue, feelings, and behaviors.

Train the client to analyze problems.

Determine coping-skills deficits versus performance failures.

Reconceptualize the client's distress based on different components (physiological, cognitive, affective, and behavioral) and stress phases.

Debunk any client myths about stress and the client's reactions to it.

| 2 | **Skills acquisition and rehearsal** |

Skills training

Ascertain client's preferred mode of coping and intrapersonal or interpersonal factors impeding such coping efforts.

Teach problem-focused instrumental coping skills directed at the modification, avoidance, and minimization of the impact of stressors (e.g., anxiety management, cognitive restructuring, self-instructional training, communication, assertion, problem solving, anger control, applied cue-controlled relaxation, parenting, study skills, using social supports).

Facilitate problem solving by identifying possibilities for change, considering and ranking alternative solutions, and practicing coping behavioral activities in the clinic and in vivo.

Teach emotionally focused palliative coping skills (e.g., perspective taking, selective attention-diversion procedures, adaptive modes of affective expression such as humor, relaxation, reframing the situation, acceptance skills, and spiritual rituals).

Teach clients how to use social supports effectively (i.e., how to choose, obtain, and maintain support).

Help clients develop an extensive repertoire of coping responses in order to facilitate flexible responding.

(continued)

Table 5.1
Phases of Stress-Inoculation Training (*Continued*)

Phase	Title
	Skills rehearsal and consolidation
	Develop and consolidate coping responses by means of behavioral and imagery rehearsal.
	Model coping (either live or videotape models).
	Use self-instructional training to help the client develop skills to self-regulate coping responses.
	Solicit client verbal commitment to employ specific efforts.
	Discuss possible barriers to coping behaviors and ways to anticipate and address such barriers.
3	**Application, relapse prevention, and follow-through**
	Encouraging application of coping skills in the form of stress-inoculation trials
	Prepare the client for application of learned skills by using coping imagery, together with techniques to identify early cues of stress.
	Expose the client, in-session, to graded stressors via imagery, and behavioral exposure to stressful and arousing scenes.
	Use graded exposure and other response induction aids to foster in vivo responding.
	Employ relapse prevention procedures (i.e., identify high-risk situations, anticipate possible stressful reactions, and rehearse coping responses).
	Use counterattitudinal procedures to increase likelihood of treatment adherence.
	Bolster self-efficacy by reviewing both the client's successful and unsuccessful coping efforts.
	Maintenance and generalization
	Gradually phase out treatment and include booster and follow-up sessions.
	Involve significant others in training, as well as peer-support and self-help groups.
	Have the client coach someone with a similar problem.
	Help the client to restructure environmental stressors and develop appropriate escape routes.
	Help the client to develop coping strategies to recover from failures and setbacks, so that lapses do not become relapses.
	Work with the client to avoid revictimization.

Note. Data from Meichenbaum (1985).

Phase 1: Conceptualization

The first phase of SIT, *conceptualization*, is designed to prepare the client for treatment and includes an educational component from which he or she can better understand the nature and origin of his or her stress and related emotions (e.g., fear, anxiety, depression). In collaboration with the client, the therapist identifies the determinants of the client's presenting clinical problems through interviews with the client and significant others, the use of an imagery-based reconstruction and assessment of a prototypical stressful incident (i.e., asking the client to vividly recount an incident that typically elicits stress for the client), psychological and situational (i.e., placing the client in stressful situations to observe his or her reaction) assessments, and behavioral observations. The client and therapist also establish short-term, intermediate, and long-term behaviorally specific goals. Self-monitoring is used to determine the client's stress-engendering appraisals (i.e., how he or she perceives the event and his or her capacity to cope with it), internal dialogue (i.e., self-talk), feelings, and behaviors, and the degree to which coping difficulties arise from *coping skills deficits* versus *performance failures* (i.e., difficulties using skills when needed). Finally myths concerning stress and coping, such as the notion that people go through uniform emotional stages of reaction in response to stress and that there is a *right* way to cope, are debunked.

Phase 2: Skills Acquisition and Rehearsal

In this phase of SIT, clients are taught a variety of coping skills to address stress, anxiety, fear, and anger in terms of physiological, behavioral, and cognitive–emotional functioning. Clients are taught how to change stressful situations when possible, the meaning of situations, and/or their emotional reactions to situations. Both problem-focused instrumental and emotion-focused palliative coping skills are taught.

Problem-focused, instrumental coping skills are directed at modification, avoidance, and minimization of the impact of stressors. Relaxation training, self-instructional or guided self-dialogue, problem-solving, attention diversion, interpersonal, and other individually tailored skills are taught in this phase. With regard to problem solving, clients are taught to identify possibilities for change, consider and rank alternative solutions, and practice coping behavioral activities in-session and in vivo. Emotion-focused palliative coping skills are taught in order for the client to have a set of skills for coping with unchangeable and uncontrollable stressors. These coping skills include perspective taking, selective attention diversion procedures, the use of humor, relaxation, and reframing of situations.

Phase 3: Application, Relapse Prevention, and Follow-Through

In the final phase of SIT, the therapist guides the client in using imagined stressful situations and coping responses to prepare her or him to apply the acquired skills in actual stressful situations. The client is exposed, in-session, to graded stressors via imagery and role plays to further inoculate her or him to stress and to consolidate new coping strategies and behaviors. Graded in vivo exposures to client-identified stressful situations are also assigned to foster development and consolidate coping skills.

With regard to relapse prevention, clients identify high-risk situations, anticipate possible stressful reactions, and rehearse coping responses in-session. Counterattitudinal procedures (i.e., therapist asks and challenges the client to indicate where, how, and why she or he will use coping efforts) are used to increase the likelihood of application of the skills. Self-efficacy is bolstered by reviewing the client's successful and unsuccessful coping efforts, with an eye toward making internalized attributions for success or mastery experiences. Treatment sessions are gradually faded out, and booster and follow-up sessions are offered that may focus on involving significant others in training, peer-support and self-help groups, as well as helping the client to develop coping strategies for recovering from failure and setbacks, so that lapses do not become relapses.

Case Example: Don

Don, a 46-year-old man, had been experiencing PTSD symptoms for at least 35 years. He consistently avoided thoughts and images related to his childhood sexual abuse by his uncle between the ages of 8 and 11. Don had never been married and did not have any significant adult intimate relationships. In fact, he avoided relationships with both men and women, reporting at his intake assessment that he did not have any significant friendships in his childhood or adulthood. Don had a history of significant alcohol misuse dating back to his adolescence, as well as periodic self-harming behavior that included burning his wrists with a lighter. He reported chronic suicidal ideation, but without imminency at the time of his presentation. Particularly stressful situations for Don included interactions with his male boss, interactions with men and women, and especially gay men, as well as thoughts and images of sexual interactions.

Don contracted to a course of SIT, which began with specific identification of stressful situations and his reactions to those situations. He was asked to describe in detail specific stressful events, including his interactions with his boss, gay men at his work and in his neighborhood, and sexual images. There was a specific focus on the unchangeable aspects of these stressful interactions (e.g., his need to interact with his boss) and the identification of goals related to these interactions. Don agreed to self-monitor stressful situations that were occurring in his current life, as well as his cognitions, feelings, and behaviors related to these situations. His coping strategies in these situations were identified, which consisted mostly of internalizing and emotion-focused strategies such as drinking, occasionally self-harming, and distraction through computer use, watching television, and ruminating about interactions with others.

In Phase 2 of SIT, Don was taught more instrumental coping skills for current day events, including assertiveness skills to use with his boss, cognitive interventions aimed at his mind reading of others' interpretations of his behavior, and (mis)interpretations of others' behaviors (e.g., gay men were *always* sexually interested in him). He was also instructed about emotionally focused coping skills that would facilitate healthier behavioral responding. Healthy social supports in his environment that were being underutilized, including the support of his sister and her family, were identified to help facilitate his more adaptive coping. In therapy sessions, Don agreed to imagine and practice using these specific skills in stressful situations with imagery rehearsal and role plays, and the therapist modeled the skills with him. The therapist solicited his agreement to use the specific skills in anticipated events and discussed possible barriers to using the skills in these situations.

With the development of these skills, the therapist helped Don to develop a hierarchy of stressors to which he could be exposed, used imagery in session to practice the skills, and prescribed increasingly difficult in vivo situations to inoculate him against future stressful situations. One example of these highly stressful situations included going to a local restaurant known to be frequented by gay men in order for Don to practice his coping skills and to prepare for high-risk stressful situations. Don was encouraged to attend a self-help group for men who had been sexually abused to maintain his gains and to provide opportunities for him to serve as a mentor for other men who had experienced similar traumatic events. The therapist also worked with Don to anticipate events that would be particularly stressful, so that he could develop coping strategies to recover from any setbacks, which he described as asking a woman on a date and having her say no. Don and the therapist developed a particular set of coping strategies that he would use to deal with this rejection in order to protect against lapses in his stress management techniques.

SKILLS TRAINING IN AFFECTIVE AND INTERPERSONAL REGULATION

STAIR was originally developed for childhood abuse survivors to be delivered sequentially with a modified version of prolonged exposure (Foa & Rothbaum, 1998) called *narrative therapy* (NT). STAIR is intended to improve emotion regulation and interpersonal functioning to prepare clients to profit from the trauma-focused interventions involved in NT. STAIR/NT has been tested in two randomized controlled trials. The first found that, compared with a minimal attention wait list, STAIR/NT led to significant reductions in PTSD symptoms (Cloitre, Koenen, Cohen, & Han, 2002). In addition, there were significant improvements in experiencing and modulating emotions and sustained reduction in three central moods: anxiety, anger, and depression. Interpersonal problems were also significantly reduced, and role functioning in home, work, and social domains was improved. All these gains were maintained at 3- and 9-month follow-up assessments. In addition, there was continued improvement in PTSD symptoms at the 3-month assessment and continued significant improvement in interpersonal functioning at the 9-month mark.

A more recent randomized controlled trial compared STAIR/NT with supportive counseling followed by NT (Support/NT) and STAIR followed by supportive counseling (STAIR/Support) in 104 women with PTSD related to childhood trauma (Cloitre et al., 2010). Results indicated that all three conditions improved PTSD symptoms, with no difference in clinician-rated PTSD symptoms between any of the treatment conditions at any assessment, with exception of STAIR/NT showing greater improvements compared with Support/NT at the 3-month follow-up assessment. Participants who received STAIR/NT were more likely to achieve sustained and full remission of their PTSD diagnosis in comparison with the two control conditions. STAIR/NT participants also demonstrated greater and sustained improvement in anger expression than did Support/NT participants. STAIR/NT yielded better mood regulation at follow-up assessments compared with Support/NT but was not superior to STAIR/Support. Finally, STAIR/NT was superior to STAIR/Support and Support/NT at follow-up assessments in terms of improvements in interpersonal problems.

STAIR is designed to include eight weekly hour-long sessions focused on particular skill deficits described in Chapter 4 (see Table 5.2). The protocol first focuses on psychoeducation regarding PTSD and then turns to emotion regulation coping skills. There is a subsequent focus on the identification of interpersonal goals, patterns in interpersonal relationships that impede acquisition of such goals, and cognitive skills focused on self- and other-related thoughts that interfere with the development and maintenance of healthy interpersonal skills.

Psychoeducation

The goals of the first session of STAIR are to increase clients' understanding of the symptoms of PTSD so that they can better understand their experience and begin to develop coping skills that can combat high levels of distress. Toward this end, clients are provided with education regarding

Table 5.2

Session-by-Session Guide to Skills Training in Affective and Interpersonal Regulation

Session	Session title and key interventions	Homework
1	Introduction to treatment	
	Psychoeducation about PTSD Treatment overview and goals Breathing retraining	Breathing retraining practice for 5 minutes twice per day
2	Identification and labeling of feelings	
	Psychoeducation about the impact of trauma on emotion regulation Introduce and practice of self- monitoring	Breathing retraining practice Daily use of the self-monitoring form
3	Emotion regulation	
	Psychoeducation about the connec- tion between feelings, thoughts, and behaviors Identification of strengths and weak- nesses in coping Tailoring and practicing new coping skills	Breathing retraining practice Self-monitoring Practice new coping skills
4	Distress tolerance	
	Psychoeducation about acceptance of feelings/distress tolerance Assess pros and cons of tolerating distress	Breathing retraining practice Self-monitoring Assess pros and cons of entering one dif- ficult situation and tolerating distress Use new skills to manage distress Engage in pleasurable activities
5	Relationship between affective and interpersonal problems	
	Psychoeducation about interpersonal schemas Introduce interpersonal schema work- sheet	Self-monitoring Practice new coping skills Pleasurable activity scheduling Interpersonal schema worksheet once daily
6	Alternative interperonal schemas	
	Psychoeducation on role-play Identify relevant interpersonal situa- tions and conduct role-plays Generate alternative schema	Self-monitoring Practice new coping skills Complete the interpersonal schema worksheet once daily Practice using alternative approach in at least one interpersonal situation

| | **Table 5.2** | |
	Session-by-Session Guide to Skills Training in Affective and Interpersonal Regulation (*Continued*)	
Session	Session title and key interventions	Homework
7	Assertiveness and control	
	Psychoeducation about assertiveness	Self-monitoring
	Discuss alternative schemas and behavioral responses	Interpersonal schema worksheet once daily
	Conduct role-plays requiring assertiveness	Practice using assertiveness in at least one interpersonal situation
	Generate alternative schemas	
8	Interpersonal flexibility	
	Psychoeducation about flexibility in interpersonal relationships	Self-monitoring
	Discuss alternative schemas and behavioral responses	Interpersonal schema worksheet once daily
	Conduct role-plays requiring flexibility	Practice using interpersonal flexibility
	Generate alternative schemas	Make list of questions/concerns regarding narrative therapy phase of treatment
	Discuss transition from Phase 1 to Phase 2 of treatment	

Note. Data from Cloitre, Cohen, and Koenen (2006).

the symptom clusters of PTSD and taught diaphragmatic breathing skills. Homework consists of practicing the breathing skills for 5 minutes, twice daily.

Emotion Regulation Skills

In the second session, clients are educated about different types of emotions and asked to self-monitor their feelings, triggers, thoughts, and coping strategies using a specific form. The developers of STAIR noted that clients inclined toward emotional numbing may need additional help to identify problematic feelings and the ways in which they minimize these feelings (Cloitre et al., 2006). Suggestions regarding new ways of coping are not made in this session. Instead, the goal is for the therapist and client to increase understanding of the client's typical methods of coping with negative emotions.

The third session of STAIR is designed to help clients identify and develop skills for coping with difficult thoughts, feelings, and behaviors. As clients learn to label feelings, thoughts, and maladaptive coping strategies, the next step is to develop more effective coping skills for dealing with distressing emotions. The client's strengths and weaknesses in each of these three areas of functioning (i.e., feelings, thoughts, coping strategies) are identified, and new adaptive coping skills are introduced. Skills are then matched to the strength/weakness profile of the client. For example, behavioral interventions aimed at increasing social support might be used with a client who tends toward social isolation. Another client might be encouraged to use self-statements to counter negative thoughts. Homework assignments are tailored to the client, and self-monitoring forms are provided to encourage the continued practice of diaphragmatic breathing.

The goal of the fourth session is to motivate clients to face distressing situations that are ultimately of value to them. Psychoeducation about the long-term negative consequences of avoidance is provided, and the idea of tolerating versus avoiding emotions is introduced. Circumstances valued by the client that make tolerating versus avoiding emotions worthwhile for longer term functioning and goal attainment are identified. As homework assignments, clients are asked to continue to practice diaphragmatic breathing, self-monitoring of emotional distress, and engaging in pleasurable activities. Related to the aim of the session, they are also asked to brainstorm the pros and cons of facing difficult but valued situations and tolerating distress.

Interpersonal Skills

After clients learn to label feelings, triggers, thoughts, and better coping responses, the protocol turns to psychoeducation about interpersonal schemas, identification of relevant schemas, and elaboration of alternative ways of perceiving self and others in interpersonal situations. Sessions five to eight are designed to help clients change negative and maladaptive interpersonal patterns so they engage with others in healthier ways. Clients identify and alter distorted interpersonal patterns by using *Interpersonal Schema Sheets* and in-session role plays.

Case Example: Don

The following discussion of the use of STAIR is based on the case information related to Don, described earlier. Both STAIR and SIT are treatments designed to be given in isolation. We simply use the same case to illustrate these interventions on a common case. Don was provided psychoeducation about the symptoms of PTSD, the goals of STAIR to improve emotion regulation and interpersonal skills, and the use of diaphragmatic breathing to regulate emotions. He successfully self-monitored his coping strategies in the face of negative emotions, which included predominant use of avoidant coping strategies such as distraction with television, computer use, and rumination. Recognizing this behavioral tendency, he was provided psychoeducation about the connections among feelings, thoughts, and behaviors, and he agreed to self-monitor daily events to become more aware of the related thoughts and emotions. For example, he self-monitored about walking through his neighborhood, thinking that gay men were "eyeing him" to have sex and his related feeling of anger.

Don was provided psychoeducation about acceptance of feelings and distress tolerance strategies, and directed to assess the pros and cons of tolerating distress in valued situations. He noted that he enjoyed many aspects of his neighborhood, including the artistic and cultural offerings in the area, which had led him to choose to reside in the neighborhood. Given this, he was assigned the activity of attending a pleasurable activity in the area (e.g., a concert) in an effort to practice skills in managing distress while engaging in a pleasurable activity.

With regard to interpersonal relationships, Don was provided psychoeducation about different beliefs about being in relation to others, and he was asked to self-monitor these types of beliefs in his current life. He was also instructed about coping skills that he could use in these situations. He chose to focus on his interactions with his boss, a situation that was used as material for a role play within treatment. He was instructed to use assertiveness skills, and specifically share his thoughts with his boss about how a particular aspect of his work could be improved. In conjunction with this role play, he generated alternative thoughts about the interaction with his boss, which included the notion that his boss might be appreciative of his efforts to improve the efficiency of their workplace. As a result of these efforts in session, Don agreed to practice the alternative behavior with his boss, and he reported success with his assertive behavior in the following session. Expanding on this success, there was discussion about flexible responding in interpersonal relationships, and he was asked to role play a situation in which his boss might not be receptive to his suggestions. Don was also asked to consider a situation with a woman in which she might not be receptive to his offer to take her on a date. He considered specific alternative thoughts and behaviors that he might use in these situations and role played them in session prior to practicing this flexible behavior.

CONCLUSION

This chapter reviewed specific skills that have the most empirical support in managing the symptoms of PTSD. These skills include management of the stress response, improved emotion regulation, and enhanced interpersonal skills. SIT and STAIR are two treatment packages that consist of these skills-focused interventions. Symptom management interventions may be particularly good options for clients who are unwilling to do trauma-focused treatments. They may also be appropriate for clients who have comorbid conditions or clinical problems that render them inappropriate for these treatments based on current evidence (e.g., self-harm, substance dependence, ongoing threat of physical or sexual victimization).

6

Promising Practices and Future Directions

E merging interventions and innovations in the application of existing cognitive-behavioral therapies (CBTs) represent ongoing efforts to expand the scope, efficacy, and efficiency of CBT for posttraumatic stress disorder (PTSD). Promising practices in the treatment of PTSD include couple- and family-based interventions, treatments for other conditions that have been modified for PTSD, technology-assisted interventions, and the use of pharmacological agents to enhance CBT outcomes. Each promising practice has different levels of empirical support, but all require more rigorous investigation to determine any advantages that they may confer over existing first-line CBTs for PTSD (e.g., improvements in other domains such as family and relationship functioning, lower rates of dropout, greater patient engagement). In this chapter, we review these

http://dx.doi.org/10.1037/14372-007
Treating PTSD With Cognitive-Behavioral Therapies: Interventions That Work, by C. M. Monson and P. Shnaider

promising practices and offer suggestions about future directions for investigation.

COUPLE AND FAMILY THERAPY

In recent years, couple- and family-based interventions have gained increasing support in the treatment of PTSD. These interventions were developed in response to a large body of literature showing that PTSD can exert effects on interpersonal factors, relationship satisfaction, and the general mental health of significant others (for reviews, see Lambert, Engh, Hasbun, & Holzer, 2012; Monson, Fredman, & Dekel, 2010; Renshaw, Blais, & Caska, 2011; Taft, Watkins, Stafford, Street, & Monson, 2011), as well as the recognition that family functioning can influence PTSD outcomes (Monson, Rodriguez, & Warner, 2005; Tarrier, Sommerfield, & Pilgrim, 1999). Although several couple- and family-based treatments for PTSD have emerged (e.g., Johnson, 2002; Monson & Fredman, 2012; Sautter, Glynn, Thompson, Franklin, & Han, 2009), the degree to which each has been empirically investigated and supported has differed. Given the cognitive-behavioral focus of this book and the greater empirical support for it, below we describe more specifically describe cognitive-behavioral conjoint therapy (CBCT) for PTSD (Monson & Fredman, 2012).

CBCT for PTSD is a trauma-focused, couple-based intervention that aims to reduce symptoms of PTSD while enhancing relationship functioning. It is based on cognitive-behavioral interpersonal theory of PTSD (Monson et al., 2010), which holds that each person in an intimate relationship has his or her own set of cognitive, behavioral, and emotional factors that interact and may serve to maintain or improve PTSD. Furthermore, each partner's cognitive-behavioral–emotional subsystem interacts with one another to influence the relationship milieu in which the couple exists. These interacting individual and relational factors are theorized to influence the occurrence and maintenance of PTSD, and they hold promise in promoting recovery from PTSD. CBCT for PTSD uses empirically-supported interventions (e.g., paraphrasing, sharing thoughts and feelings, cognitive interventions, behavioral approach assignments) to address individual- and relationship-level factors that contribute to PTSD and relationship problems. It is important to note that CBCT for PTSD aims to *enhance* relationship functioning and does not require couples to be in clinically distressed relationships to participate in the therapy.

Results from three uncontrolled trials and one randomized wait-list controlled trial have demonstrated the efficacy of CBCT for PTSD to consistently reduce PTSD and comorbid symptoms within community and veteran samples (Monson et al., 2011, 2012; Monson, Schnurr, Stevens, & Guthrie, 2004; Schumm, Fredman, Monson, & Chard, 2013). In addition, significant improvements in intimate relationship satisfaction have been found per patient- or partner-report. Preliminary research demonstrates that the benefits of CBCT for PTSD may extend to improvements in partners' psychological functioning (Monson, Stevens, & Schnurr, 2005; Shnaider, Pukay-Martin, Fredman, Macdonald, & Monson, in press).

BEHAVIORAL ACTIVATION

Recent studies have begun to examine the efficacy of behavioral activation (BA) for PTSD. BA was originally designed to decrease symptoms of major depressive disorder by increasing the client's participation in reinforcing activities that bring pleasure and/or mastery (Martell, Addis, & Jacobson, 2001). Given that the avoidance symptoms of PTSD are conceptualized to maintain the disorder, reengagement with activities that have been avoided, and that have the potential to increase pleasure or mastery, represents a logical extension of the application of BA to PTSD.

To date, there have been two case studies (Mulick & Naugle, 2004; Turner & Jakupcak, 2010), two uncontrolled trials (Jakupcak et al., 2006; Jakupcak, Wagner, Paulson, Varra, & McFall, 2010), and one randomized effectiveness trial (Wagner, Zatzick, Ghesquiere, & Jurkovich, 2007) examining BA for PTSD. In addition, an uncontrolled trial of a CBT treatment package consisting of BA followed by exposure therapy and cognitive restructuring for individuals with PTSD and major depressive disorder has been conducted (Nixon & Nearmy, 2011). Most of these studies have found statistically and/or clinically significant reductions in PTSD symptoms, yet depressive symptom improvements have been inconsistent. This may be because some studies recruited for clients with PTSD only and not necessarily a comorbid major depressive disorder diagnosis, potentially limiting the ability to find significant improvements in depressive symptomatology. It may also be related to modifications made to the original BA protocol when applying it to PTSD in some studies (e.g., Wagner et al., 2007), changing the focus of behavioral exercises to reduce avoidance behavior versus increasing engagement in activities that bring pleasure or mastery.

VIRTUAL REALITY EXPOSURE THERAPY

Several studies have documented the use of virtual reality technology, or immersive, real-time, computer-simulated environments that sometimes include tactile and olfactory trauma-related stimuli (e.g., smell of petroleum, vibrations similar to explosions), to enhance the treatment of anxiety disorders (for reviews, see Gerardi, Cukor, Difede, Rizzo, & Rothbaum, 2010; Parsons & Rizzo, 2008; Powers & Emmelkamp, 2008). Recent reviews of studies on virtual reality for PTSD have documented large effect size improvements in PTSD that are maintained at 6-month follow-up (e.g., Cukor, Spitalnick, Difede, Rizzo, & Rothbaum, 2009; Gerardi et al., 2010; Gonçalves, Pedrozo, Countinho, Figueira, & Ventura, 2012).

Cukor et al. (2009) argued that virtual reality presents an environment in which individuals may engage with their trauma memories in a way that is more vivid and immersive than the traditional approach used in imaginal exposures, allowing for faster and/or deeper emotional processing. In addition, it provides access to stimuli for virtual in vivo exposures that are typically prohibitive due to cost or feasibility (e.g., airplanes, improvised explosive devices, active combat scenarios). Cukor et al. also highlighted issues that may be barriers to conducting traditional exposure therapy for PTSD (e.g., avoidance of the trauma memory, lack of emotional or sensory engagement during exposures) and suggested that virtual reality exposure therapy may be a possible remedy for these problems.

PHARMACOLOGICAL AGENTS TO ENHANCE THE EFFICACY OF COGNITIVE-BEHAVIORAL THERAPIES

Currently available psychopharmacological agents have yielded relatively modest effects as a stand-alone approach to treating PTSD (for a review, see Ipser, Seedat, & Stein, 2006). However, there have been recent efforts to test medication as an adjunctive intervention to enhance the efficacy of CBT for PTSD. D-cycloserine (DCS) and hydrocortisone have been investigated in pharmacologically assisted CBT trials for PTSD.

A placebo-controlled trial of DCS-augmented prolonged exposure found that, in general, the treatment effects were not enhanced with DCS, but that participants with more severe PTSD did show additional benefits in symptom reduction by receiving DCS (de Kleine, Hendriks, Kuster, Broekman, & van Minnen, 2012). In contrast, Litz et al. (2012) examined DCS-augmented imaginal exposure for PTSD and found that those in the DCS condition actually evidenced poorer treatment outcomes. Although DCS has been found to augment the efficacy of exposure therapy for other anxiety disorders (for a review, see Norberg, Krystal, & Tolin, 2008), these initial studies do not support the augmenting power of DCS in exposure interventions for PTSD.

Similarly, two studies have tested the use of hydrocortisone to enhance CBT interventions for PTSD. Surís, North, Adinoff, Powell, and Greene (2010) used a single session, placebo-controlled intervention in which individuals wrote about two traumatic events and were then given either hydrocortisone or a placebo. There were significantly greater improvements in PTSD avoidance/numbing symptoms 1 week after the intervention for those receiving hydrocortisone. However, this difference was not maintained at the 1-month postintervention assessment. In two case studies (one in which subjects received hydrocortisone and the other, placebo alongside prolonged exposure), Yehuda, Bierer, Pratchett, and Malowney (2010) reported that the individual receiving hydrocortisone-augmented prolonged exposure evidenced a more rapid and greater improvement in PTSD symptoms compared with the individual receiving placebo-augmented prolonged exposure. Given the methodological limitations of this study, and the minimal differences found in Surís et al.'s brief intervention study, it is difficult to ascertain the potential benefits of augmentation of CBT interventions with hydrocortisone.

CONCLUSION

The continuing development and enhancement of CBTs for PTSD demonstrates an effort to help as many individuals suffering from this condition as possible. By reviewing some of the promising areas of practice, we aimed to highlight the emerging treatments being developed and tested to address PTSD and its comorbid conditions. Although all the treatments reviewed in this chapter have shown some level of empirical support in reducing symptoms of PTSD, they require additional investigation to clearly establish their efficacy, equivalence to first-line treatments, and additional benefits that may result from their use. We are hopeful that these ongoing efforts will ultimately result in a greater number of empirically supported treatments for PTSD that can be matched to clients with various clinical presentations and comorbid problems.

Appendix:
Clinician Resources

The following resources are geared toward clinicians seeking to learn more about the treatment of posttraumatic stress disorder and the cognitive-behavioral interventions described in this book.

TREATMENT MANUALS

Cloitre, M., Cohen, L. R., & Koenen, K. C. (2006). *Treating survivors of childhood abuse: Psychotherapy for the interrupted life.* New York, NY: Guilford Press.

Foa, E. B., Hembree, E. A., & Rothbaum, B. O. (2007). *Prolonged exposure therapy for PTSD: Emotional processing of traumatic experiences: Therapist guide.* New York, NY: Oxford University Press.

Meichenbaum, D. (1985). *Stress inoculation training.* Elmsford, NY: Pergamon Press.

Monson, C. M., & Fredman, S. J. (2012). *Cognitive-behavioral conjoint therapy for posttraumatic stress disorder: Harnessing the healing power of relationships.* New York, NY: Guilford Press.

Resick, P. A., Monson, C. M., & Chard, K. M. (2008). *Cognitive processing therapy: Veteran/military version.* Washington, DC: Department of Veterans Affairs.

BOOKS

Beck, J. G., & Sloan, D. M. (Eds.). (2012). *The Oxford handbook of traumatic stress disorders.* New York, NY: Oxford University Press.

Foa, E. B., Keane, T. M., Friedman, M. J., & Cohen, J. A. (Eds.). (2009). *Effective treatments for PTSD: Practice guidelines from the International Society for Traumatic Stress Studies* (2nd ed.). New York, NY: Guilford Press.

Follette, V. M., & Ruzek, J. I. (Eds.). (2006). *Cognitive behavioral therapies for trauma* (2nd ed.). New York, NY: Guilford Press.

Friedman, M. J., Keane, T. M., & Resick, P. A. (Eds.). (2007). *Handbook of PTSD: Science and practice.* New York, NY: Guilford Press.

Zayfert, C., & Becker, C. B. (2007). *Cognitive-behavioral therapy for PTSD: A case formulation approach.* New York, NY: Guilford Press.

WEBSITES

Australian Centre for Posttraumatic Mental Health
http://www.acpmh.unimelb.edu.au

Couple Therapy for PTSD: A Community of Practice for Therapists
http://www.coupletherapyforptsd.com

Cognitive Processing Therapy for Posttraumatic Stress Disorder
http://www.cptforptsd.com

International Society for Traumatic Stress Studies
http://www.istss.org

Center for the Treatment and Study of Anxiety
http://www.med.upenn.edu/ctsa/ptsd.html

United States Department of Veterans Affairs: National Center for PTSD
http://www.ptsd.va.gov

National Institute for Health and Care Excellence
http://www.nice.org.uk/CG26

References

Abramowitz, J. S., Deacon, B. J., & Whiteside, S. P. H. (2010). *Exposure therapy for anxiety: Principles and practice.* New York, NY: Guilford Press.

Abramowitz, J. S., Franklin, M. E., Zoellner, L. A., & Dibernardo, C. L. (2002). Treatment compliance and outcome in obsessive-compulsive disorder. *Behavior Modification, 26,* 447–463. doi:10.1177/0145445502026004001

Addis, M. E., & Jacobson, N. S. (2000). A closer look at treatment rationale and homework compliance in cognitive–behavioral therapy for depression. *Cognitive Therapy and Research, 24,* 313–326. doi:10.1023/A:1005563304265

American Psychiatric Association. (2004). *Practice guidelines for the treatment of patients with acute stress disorder and posttraumatic stress disorder.* http://dx.doi.org/10.1176/appi.books.9780890423363.52257

Anderson, H., & Goolishian, H. (1992). The client is the expert: A not-knowing approach to therapy. In S. McNamee & K. J. Gergen (Eds.), *Therapy as social construction* (pp. 25–39). London, United Kingdom: Sage.

Antony, M. M., & Roemer, L. (2011). *Behavior therapy.* Washington, DC: American Psychological Association.

Antony, M. M., & Swinson, R. P. (2000). *Phobic disorders and panic in adults: A guide to assessment and treatment.* Washington, DC: American Psychological Association. doi:10.1037/10348-000

Australian Centre for Posttraumatic Mental Health. (2007). *Australian guidelines for the treatment of adults with acute stress disorder and posttraumatic stress disorder.* Carlton, Australia: Australian Centre for Posttraumatic Mental Health.

Başoğlu, M., Şalcioğlu, E., Livanou, M., Kalender, D., & Acar, G. (2005). Single-session behavioral treatment for earthquake-related posttraumatic stress disorder: A randomized waiting list controlled trial. *Journal of Traumatic Stress, 18,* 1–11. doi:10.1002/jts.20011

Beck, A. T. (1979). *Cognitive therapy of depression.* New York, NY: Guilford Press.

Beck, A. T., Emery, G., & Greenberg, R. L. (2005). *Anxiety disorders and phobias: A cognitive perspective.* Cambridge, MA: Basic Books.

Beck, J. G., Gudmundsdottir, B., Palyo, S. A., Miller, L. M., & Grant, D. M. (2006). Rebound effects following deliberate thought suppression: Does PTSD make a difference? *Behavior Therapy, 37,* 170–180. doi:10.1016/j.beth.2005.11.002

Becker, C. B., Zayfert, C., & Anderson, E. (2004). A survey of psychologists' attitudes towards and utilization of exposure therapy for PTSD. *Behaviour Research and Therapy, 42,* 277–292. doi:10.1016/S0005-7967(03)00138-4

Bishop, W., & Fish, J. M. (1999). Questions as interventions: Perceptions of Socratic, solution focused, and diagnostic questioning styles. *Journal of Rational-Emotive & Cognitive-Behavior Therapy, 17,* 115–140. doi:10.1023/A:1023005015329

Bisson, J., & Andrew, M. (2009). Psychological treatment of post-traumatic stress disorder (PTSD). *Cochrane Database of Systematic Reviews, 2007*(3), 1–48. doi:10.1002/14651858.CD003388.pub3

Bisson, J. I., Ehlers, A., Matthews, R., Pilling, S., Richards, D., & Turner, S. (2007). Psychological treatments for chronic post-traumatic stress disorder: Systematic review and meta-analysis. *British Journal of Psychiatry, 190,* 97–104. doi:10.1192/bjp.bp.106.021402

Bolten, H. (2001). Managers develop moral accountability: The impact of Socratic dialogue. *Reason in Practice, 1*(3), 21–34. doi:10.5840/pom2001134

Boudewyns, P. A., & Hyer, L. (1990). Physiological response to combat memories and preliminary treatment outcome in Vietnam veteran PTSD patients treated with direct therapeutic exposure. *Behavior Therapy, 21,* 63–87. doi:10.1016/S0005-7894(05)80189-3

Bouton, M. E. (2000). A learning theory perspective on lapse, relapse, and the maintenance of behavior change. *Health Psychology, 19,* 57–63. doi:10.1037/0278-6133.19.Suppl1.57

Bouton, M. E. (2004). Context and behavioral processes in extinction. *Learning & Memory, 11,* 485–494. doi:10.1101/lm.78804

Bowlby, J. (1982). *Attachment and loss: Vol. 1. Attachment* (2nd ed.). New York, NY: Basic Books. (Original work published 1969).

Bradley, R., Greene, J., Russ, E., Dutra, L., & Westen, D. (2005). A multidimensional meta-analysis of psychotherapy for PTSD. *American Journal of Psychiatry, 162,* 214–227. doi:10.1176/appi.ajp.162.2.214

Briere, J. (1988). The long-term clinical correlates of childhood sexual victimization. In R. A. Prentky & V. L. Quinsey (Eds.), *Annals of the New York Academy of Sciences: Vol. 528. Human sexual aggression: Current perspectives* (pp. 327–334). doi:10.1111/j.1749-6632.1988.tb50874.x

Bryant, R. A., & Harvey, A. G. (2002). Delayed-onset posttraumatic stress disorder: A prospective evaluation. *Australian and New Zealand Journal of Psychiatry, 36*, 205–209. doi:10.1046/j.1440-1614.2002.01009.x

Bryant, R. A., Moulds, M. L., Guthrie, R. M., Dang, S. T., Mastrodomenico, J., Nixon, R. D. V., . . . Creamer, M. (2008). A randomized controlled trial of exposure therapy and cognitive restructuring for posttraumatic stress disorder. *Journal of Consulting and Clinical Psychology, 76*, 695–703. doi:10.1037/a0012616

Bryant, R. A., Moulds, M. L., Guthrie, R. M., Dang, S. T., & Nixon, R. D. V. (2003). Imaginal exposure alone and imaginal exposure with cognitive restructuring in treatment of posttraumatic stress disorder. *Journal of Consulting and Clinical Psychology, 71*, 706–712. doi:10.1037/0022-006X.71.4.706

Buckley, T. C., Blanchard, E. B., & Hickling, E. J. (1996). A prospective examination of delayed onset PTSD secondary to motor vehicle accidents. *Journal of Abnormal Psychology, 105*, 617–625. doi:10.1037/0021-843X.105.4.617

Burns, D. D. (1999). *Feeling good.* New York, NY: Avon Books.

Chard, K. M. (2005). An evaluation of cognitive processing therapy for the treatment of posttraumatic stress disorder related to childhood sexual abuse. *Journal of Consulting and Clinical Psychology, 73*, 965–971. doi:10.1037/0022-006X.73.5.965

Chemtob, C. M., Novaco, R. W., Hamada, R. S., Gross, D. M., & Smith, G. (1997). Anger regulation deficits in combat-related posttraumatic stress disorder. *Journal of Traumatic Stress, 10*, 17–36. doi:10.1002/jts.2490100104

Cloitre, M., Cohen, L. R., & Koenen, K. C. (2006). *Treating survivors of childhood abuse: Psychotherapy for the interrupted life.* New York, NY: Guilford Press.

Cloitre, M., Koenen, K. C., Cohen, L. R., & Han, H. (2002). Skills training in affective and interpersonal regulation followed by exposure: A phase-based treatment for PTSD related to childhood abuse. *Journal of Consulting and Clinical Psychology, 70*, 1067–1074. doi:10.1037/0022-006X.70.5.1067

Cloitre, M., Miranda, R., Stovall-McClough, K. C., & Han, H. (2005). Beyond PTSD: Emotion regulation and interpersonal problems as predictors of functional impairment in survivors of childhood abuse. *Behavior Therapy, 36*, 119–124. doi:10.1016/S0005-7894(05)80060-7

Cloitre, M., Stovall-McClough, K. C., Nooner, K., Zorbas, P., Cherry, S., Jackson, C. L., . . . Petkova, E. (2010). Treatment for PTSD related to childhood abuse: A randomized controlled trial. *American Journal of Psychiatry, 167*, 915–924. doi:10.1176/appi.ajp.2010.09081247

Cloitre, M., Stovall-McClough, K. C., Zorbas, P., & Charuvastra, A. (2008). Attachment organization, emotion regulation, and expectations of support in a clinical sample of women with childhood abuse histories. *Journal of Traumatic Stress, 21*, 282–289. doi:10.1002/jts.20339

Cooper, N. A., & Clum, G. A. (1989). Imaginal flooding as a supplementary treatment for PTSD in combat veterans: A controlled study. *Behavior Therapy, 20*, 381–391. doi:10.1016/S0005-7894(89)80057-7

Craske, M. G., Kircanski, K., Zelikowsky, M., Mystkowski, J., Chowdhury, N., & Baker, A. (2008). Optimizing inhibitory learning during exposure therapy. *Behaviour Research and Therapy, 46*, 5–27. doi:10.1016/j.brat.2007.10.003

Cukor, J., Spitalnick, J., Difede, J., Rizzo, A., & Rothbaum, B. O. (2009). Emerging treatments for PTSD. *Clinical Psychology Review, 29*, 715–726. doi:10.1016/j.cpr.2009.09.001

de Kleine, R. A., Hendriks, G. J., Kuster, W. J. C., Broekman, T. G., & van Minnen, A. (2012). A randomized placebo-controlled trial of D-cycloserine to enhance exposure therapy for posttraumatic stress disorder. *Biological Psychiatry, 71*, 962–968. doi:10.1016/j.biopsych.2012.02.033

Deveney, C. M., & Deldin, P. J. (2006). A preliminary investigation of cognitive flexibility for emotional information in major depressive disorder and nonpsychiatric controls. *Emotion, 6*, 429–437. doi:10.1037/1528-3542.6.3.429

Ehlers, A., Bisson, J., Clark, D. M., Creamer, M., Pilling, S., Richards, D., . . . Yule, W. (2010). Do all psychological treatments really work the same in posttraumatic stress disorder? *Clinical Psychology Review, 30*, 269–276. doi:10.1016/j.cpr.2009.12.001

Ehlers, A., & Clark, D. M. (2000). A cognitive model of posttraumatic stress disorder. *Behaviour Research and Therapy, 38*, 319–345. doi:10.1016/S0005-7967(99)00123-0

Ehlers, A., Clark, D. M., Hackmann, A., McManus, F., & Fennell, M. (2005). Cognitive therapy for post-traumatic stress disorder: Development and evaluation. *Behaviour Research and Therapy, 43*, 413–431. doi:10.1016/j.brat.2004.03.006

Ehlers, A., Mayou, R. A., & Bryant, B. (1998). Psychological predictors of chronic posttraumatic stress disorder after motor vehicle accidents. *Journal of Abnormal Psychology, 107*, 508–519. doi:10.1037/0021-843X.107.3.508

Elder, L., & Paul, R. (1998). The role of Socratic questioning in thinking, teaching, and learning. *Clearing House: A Journal of Educational Strategies, Issues and Ideas, 71*, 297–301. doi:10.1080/00098659809602729

Feeny, N. C., Hembree, E. A., & Zoellner, L. A. (2003). Myths regarding exposure therapy for PTSD. *Cognitive and Behavioral Practice, 10*, 85–90. doi:10.1016/S1077-7229(03)80011-1

Feske, U. (2008). Treating low-income and minority women with posttraumatic stress disorder: A pilot study comparing prolonged exposure and treatment as usual conducted by community therapists. *Journal of Interpersonal Violence, 23*, 1027–1040. doi:10.1177/0886260507313967

Fischhoff, B. (1975). Hindsight ≠ foresight: The effect of outcome knowledge on judgment under uncertainty. *Journal of Experimental Psychology: Human Perception and Performance, 1*, 288–299. doi:10.1037/0096-1523.1.3.288

Foa, E. B., Dancu, C. V., Hembree, E. A., Jaycox, L. H., Meadows, E. A., & Street, G. P. (1999). A comparison of exposure therapy, stress inoculation training, and their combination for reducing posttraumatic stress disorder in female assault victims. *Journal of Consulting and Clinical Psychology, 67*, 194–200. doi:10.1037/0022-006X.67.2.194

Foa, E. B., Hembree, E. A., & Rothbaum, B. O. (2007). *Prolonged exposure therapy for PTSD: Emotional processing of traumatic experiences: Therapist guide.* New York, NY: Oxford University Press.

Foa, E. B., Huppert, J. D., & Cahill, S. P. (2006). Emotional processing theory: An update. In B. O. Rothbaum (Ed.), *Pathological anxiety: Emotional processing in etiology and treatment* (pp. 3–24). New York, NY: Guilford Press.

Foa, E. B., Keane, T. M., Friedman, M. J., & Cohen, J. A. (Eds.). (2009). *Effective treatments for PTSD: Practice guidelines from the International Society for Traumatic Stress Studies* (2nd ed.). New York, NY: Guilford Press.

Foa, E. B., & Kozak, M. J. (1986). Emotional processing of fear: Exposure to corrective information. *Psychological Bulletin, 99*, 20–35. doi:10.1037/0033-2909.99.1.20

Foa, E. B., & McNally, R. J. (1996). Mechanisms of change in exposure therapy. In R. Rapee (Ed.), *Current controversies in the anxiety disorders* (pp. 329–343). New York, NY: Guilford Press.

Foa, E. B., & Rauch, S. A. (2004). Cognitive changes during prolonged exposure versus prolonged exposure plus cognitive restructuring in female assault survivors with posttraumatic stress disorder. *Journal of Consulting and Clinical Psychology, 72*, 879–884. doi:10.1037/0022-006X.72.5.879

Foa, E. B., Riggs, D. S., Massie, E. D., & Yarczower, M. (1995). The impact of fear activation and anger on the efficacy of exposure treatment for posttraumatic stress disorder. *Behavior Therapy, 26*, 487–499. doi:10.1016/S0005-7894(05)80096-6

Foa, E. B., & Rothbaum, B. O. (1998). *Treating the trauma of rape.* New York, NY: Guilford Press.

Foa, E. B., Rothbaum, B. O., Riggs, D. S., & Murdock, T. B. (1991). Treatment of posttraumatic stress disorder in rape victims: A comparison between cognitive–behavioral procedures and counseling. *Journal of Consulting and Clinical Psychology, 59*, 715–723. doi:10.1037/0022-006X.59.5.715

Forbes, D., Lloyd, D., Nixon, R. D. V., Elliot, P., Varker, T., Perry, D., . . . Creamer, M. (2012). A multisite randomized controlled effectiveness trial of cognitive processing therapy for military-related posttraumatic stress disorder. *Journal of Anxiety Disorders, 26*, 442–452. doi:10.1016/j.janxdis.2012.01.006

Freyd, J. J. (1996). *Betrayal trauma: The logic of forgetting childhood abuse.* Cambridge, MA: Harvard University Press.

Galovski, T. E., Blain, L. M., Mott, J. M., Elwood, L., & Houle, T. (2012). Manualized therapy for PTSD: Flexing the structure of cognitive processing therapy. *Journal of Consulting and Clinical Psychology, 80,* 968–981. doi:10.1037/a0030600

Galovski, T. E., Monson, C. M., Bruce, S. E., & Resick, P. A. (2009). Does cognitive–behavioral therapy for PTSD improve perceived health and sleep impairment? *Journal of Traumatic Stress, 22,* 197–204. doi:10.1002/jts.20418

Gerardi, M., Cukor, J., Difede, J., Rizzo, A., & Rothbaum, B. O. (2010). Virtual reality exposure therapy for post-traumatic stress disorder and other anxiety disorders. *Current Psychiatry Reports, 12,* 298–305. doi:10.1007/s11920-010-0128-4

Germain, V., Marchand, A., Bouchard, S., Drouin, M. S., & Guay, S. (2009). Effectiveness of cognitive behavioural therapy administered by videoconferencing for posttraumatic stress disorder. *Cognitive Behaviour Therapy, 38,* 42–53. doi:10.1080/16506070802473494

Gonçalves, R., Pedrozo, A. L., Countinho, E. S. F., Figueira, I., & Ventura, P. (2012). Efficacy of virtual reality exposure therapy in the treatment of PTSD: A systematic review. *PLoS ONE, 7,* e48469. doi:10.1371/journal.pone.0048469

Grey, N., & Holmes, E. A. (2008). "Hotspots" in trauma memories in the treatment of post-traumatic stress disorder: A replication. *Memory, 16,* 788–796. doi:10.1080/09658210802266446

Hirai, M., & Clum, G. A. (2005). An Internet-based self-change program for traumatic event related fear, distress, and maladaptive coping. *Journal of Traumatic Stress, 18,* 631–636. doi:10.1002/jts.20071

Holmes, E. A., Grey, N., & Young, K. A. D. (2005). Intrusive images and "hotspots" of trauma memories in posttraumatic stress disorder: An exploratory investigation of emotions and cognitive themes. *Journal of Behavior Therapy and Experimental Psychiatry, 36,* 3–17. doi:10.1016/j.jbtep.2004.11.002

Ipser, J., Seedat, A., & Stein, D. J. (2006). Pharmacotherapy for post-traumatic stress disorder—A systematic review and meta-analysis. *South African Medical Journal, 96,* 1088–1096.

Jakupcak, M., Roberts, L. J., Martell, C., Mulick, P., Michael, S., Reed, R., . . . McFall, M. (2006). A pilot study of behavioral activation for veterans with posttraumatic stress disorder. *Journal of Traumatic Stress, 19,* 387–391. doi:10.1002/jts.20125

Jakupcak, M., Wagner, A., Paulson, A., Varra, A., & McFall, M. (2010). Behavioral activation as a primary care-based treatment for PTSD and depression among returning veterans. *Journal of Traumatic Stress, 23,* 491–495. doi:10.1002/jts.20543

Janoff-Bulman, R. (1989). Assumptive worlds and the stress of traumatic events: Applications of the schema construct. *Social Cognition, 7*, 113–136. doi:10.1521/soco.1989.7.2.113

Janoff-Bulman, R. (2010). *Shattered assumptions.* New York, NY: Free Press.

Jaycox, L. H., Foa, E. B., & Morral, A. R. (1998). Influence of emotional engagement and habituation on exposure therapy for PTSD. *Journal of Consulting and Clinical Psychology, 66*, 185–192. doi:10.1037/0022-006X.66.1.185

Johnson, S. M. (2002). *Emotionally focused couple therapy with trauma survivors: Strengthening attachment bonds.* New York, NY: Guilford Press.

Keane, T. M., Fairbank, J. A., Caddell, J. M., & Zimfring, R. T. (1989). Implosive (flooding) therapy reduces symptoms of PTSD in Vietnam combat veterans. *Behavior Therapy, 20*, 245–260. doi:10.1016/S0005-7894(89)80072-3

Knaevelsrud, C., & Maercker, A. (2007). Internet-based treatment for PTSD reduces distress and facilitates the development of a strong therapeutic alliance: A randomized controlled clinical trial. *BMC Psychiatry, 7*, Article 13. doi:10.1186/1471-244X-7-13

Lambert, J. E., Engh, R., Hasbun, A., & Holzer, J. (2012). Impact of posttraumatic stress disorder on the relationship quality and psychological distress of intimate partners: A meta-analytic review. *Journal of Family Psychology, 26*, 729–737. doi:10.1037/a0029341

Lang, P. J. (1977). Imagery in therapy: An information processing analysis of fear. *Behavior Therapy, 8*, 862–886. doi:10.1016/S0005-7894(77)80157-3

Lang, P. J. (1979). A bio-informational theory of emotional imagery. *Psychophysiology, 16*, 495–512. doi:10.1111/j.1469-8986.1979.tb01511.x

Lange, A., van de Ven, J.-P., & Schrieken, B. (2003). Interapy: Treatment of posttraumatic stress via the Internet. *Cognitive Behaviour Therapy, 32*, 110–124. doi:10.1080/16506070302317

Lazarus, R. S., & Folkman, S. (1984). *Stress, appraisal, and coping.* New York, NY: Springer.

Lerner, M. J. (1980). *The belief in a just world: A fundamental delusion.* New York, NY: Plenum Press. doi:10.1007/978-1-4899-0448-5

Litz, B. T., Engel, C. C., Bryant, R. A., & Papa, A. (2007). A randomized controlled proof-of-concept trial of an Internet-based, therapist assisted self-management treatment for posttraumatic stress disorder. *American Journal of Psychiatry, 164*, 1676–1683. doi:10.1176/appi.ajp.2007.06122057

Litz, B. T., & Keane, T. M. (1989). Information processing in anxiety disorders: An application to the understanding of post-traumatic stress disorder. *Clinical Psychology Review, 9*, 243–257. doi:10.1016/0272-7358(89)90030-5

Litz, B. T., Salters-Pedneault, K., Steenkamp, M. M., Hermos, J. A., Bryant, R. A., Otto, M. W., & Hofmann, S. G. (2012). A randomized placebo-controlled trial of D-cycloserine and exposure therapy for posttraumatic stress disorder. *Journal of Psychiatric Research, 46*, 1184–1190. doi:10.1016/j.jpsychires.2012.05.006

Lyons, J. A., & Keane, T. M. (1989). Implosive therapy for the treatment of combat-related PTSD. *Journal of Traumatic Stress, 2*, 137–152. doi:10.1002/jts.2490020203

Management of Post-Traumatic Stress Working Group. (2010). *VA/DoD clinical practice guideline for management of post-traumatic stress.* Washington, DC: Department of Veterans Affairs and Department of Defense.

Marks, I., Lovell, K., Noshirvani, H., Livanou, M., & Thrasher, S. (1998). Treatment of posttraumatic stress disorder by exposure and/or cognitive restructuring: A controlled study. *Archives of General Psychiatry, 55*, 317–325. doi:10.1001/archpsyc.55.4.317

Martell, C. R., Addis, M. E., & Jacobson, N. S. (2001). *Depression in context: Strategies for guided action.* New York, NY: Norton.

McCann, I. L., & Pearlman, L. A. (1990). *Psychological trauma and the adult survivor: Theory, therapy, and transformation.* Philadelphia, PA: Brunner/Mazel.

McGuire, W. J. (1964). Inducing resistance to persuasion: Some contemporary approaches. *Advances in Experimental Social Psychology, 1*, 191–229.

Meichenbaum, D. (1985). *Stress inoculation training.* Elmsford, NY: Pergamon Press.

Meichenbaum, D. (2007). Stress inoculation training: A preventative and treatment approach. In P. M. Lehrer, R. L. Woolfolk, & W. S. Sime (Eds.), *Principles and practice of stress management* (pp. 497–518). New York, NY: Guilford Press.

Meichenbaum, D., & Fitzpatrick, D. (1993). A narrative constructivist perspective of stress and coping: Stress inoculation applications. In L. Goldberger & S. Breznitz (Eds.), *Handbook of stress: Theoretical and clinical aspects* (2nd ed., pp. 706–723). New York, NY: Free Press.

Meuret, A. E., Wilhelm, F. H., Ritz, T., & Roth, W. T. (2003). Breathing training for treating panic disorder: Useful intervention or impediment? *Behavior Modification, 27*, 731–754. doi:10.1177/0145445503256324

Monson, C. M., & Fredman, S. J. (2012). *Cognitive–behavioral conjoint therapy for posttraumatic stress disorder: Harnessing the healing power of relationships.* New York, NY: Guilford Press.

Monson, C. M., Fredman, S. J., Adair, K. C., Stevens, S. P., Resick, P. A., Schnurr, P. P., . . . Macdonald, A. (2011). Cognitive–behavioral conjoint therapy for PTSD: Pilot results from a community sample. *Journal of Traumatic Stress, 24*, 97–101. doi:10.1002/jts.20604

Monson, C. M., Fredman, S. J., & Dekel, R. (2010). Posttraumatic stress disorder in an interpersonal context. In J. G. Beck (Ed.), *Interpersonal processes in the anxiety disorders: Implications for understanding psychopathology and treatment* (pp. 179–208). Washington, DC: American Psychological Association. doi:10.1037/12084-007

Monson, C. M., Fredman, S. J., Macdonald, A., Pukay-Martin, N. D., Resick, P. A., & Schnurr, P. P. (2012). Effects of cognitive–behavioral couple therapy for PTSD: A randomized controlled trial. *JAMA, 308*, 700–709. doi:10.1001/jama.2012.9307

Monson, C. M., Price, J. A., Rodriguez, B. F., Ripley, M. P., & Warner, R. A. (2004). Emotional deficits in military-related PTSD: An investigation of content and process disturbances. *Journal of Traumatic Stress, 17*, 275–279. doi:10.1023/B:JOTS.0000029271.58494.05

Monson, C. M., Rodriguez, B. F., & Warner, R. (2005). Cognitive–behavioral therapy for PTSD in the real world: Do interpersonal relationships make a real difference? *Journal of Clinical Psychology, 61*, 751–761. doi:10.1002/jclp.20096

Monson, C. M., Schnurr, P. P., Resick, P. A., Friedman, M. J., Young-Xu, Y., & Stevens, S. P. (2006). Cognitive processing therapy for veterans with military-related posttraumatic stress disorder. *Journal of Consulting and Clinical Psychology, 74*, 898–907. doi:10.1037/0022-006X.74.5.898

Monson, C. M., Schnurr, P. P., Stevens, S. P., & Guthrie, K. A. (2004). Cognitive–behavioral couple's treatment for posttraumatic stress disorder: Initial findings. *Journal of Traumatic Stress, 17*, 341–344. doi:10.1023/B:JOTS. 0000038483.69570.5b

Monson, C. M., Stevens, S. P., & Schnurr, P. P. (2005). Cognitive–behavioral couple's treatment for posttraumatic stress disorder. In T. A. Corales (Ed.), *Focus on posttraumatic stress disorder research* (pp. 245–274). Hauppauge, NY: Nova Science.

Mowrer, O. H. (1960). *Learning theory and behavior.* (Vol. 960). New York, NY: John Wiley & Sons. doi:10.1037/10802-000

Mulick, P. S., & Naugle, A. E. (2004). Behavioral activation for comorbid PTSD and major depression: A case study. *Cognitive and Behavioral Practice, 11*, 378–387. doi:10.1016/S1077-7229(04)80054-3

Najavits, L. M. (2002). *Seeking safety: A treatment manual for PTSD and substance abuse.* New York, NY: Guilford Press.

National Institute for Health and Care Excellence. (2005). *Clinical guideline 26: Posttraumatic stress disorder (PTSD): The management of PTSD in adults and children in primary and secondary care.* London, United Kingdom: National Collaborating Centre for Mental Health.

Nixon, R. D., & Nearmy, D. M. (2011). Treatment of comorbid posttraumatic stress disorder and major depressive disorder: A pilot study. *Journal of Traumatic Stress, 24*, 451–455. doi:10.1002/jts.20654

Nixon, R. D., Nishith, P., & Resick, P. A. (2004). The accumulative effect of trauma exposure on short-term and delayed verbal memory in a treatment-seeking sample of female rape victims. *Journal of Traumatic Stress, 17,* 31–35. doi:10.1023/B:JOTS.0000014673.02925.db

Norberg, M. M., Krystal, J. H., & Tolin, D. F. (2008). A meta-analysis of D-cycloserine and the facilitation of fear extinction and exposure therapy. *Biological Psychiatry, 63,* 1118–1126. doi:10.1016/j.biopsych.2008.01.012

Novaco, R. W. (1983). *Stress inoculation therapy for anger control: A manual for therapists.* Unpublished manuscript, University of California, Irvine.

O'Connor, A. M., Bennett, C. L., Stacey, D., Barry, M., Col, N. F., Eden, K. B., . . . Rover, D. (2009). Decision aids for people facing health treatment or screening decisions. *Cochrane Database of Systematic Reviews, 2009*(3). doi:10.1002/14651858.CD001431.pub2

Padesky, C. A. (1993, September). *Socratic questioning: Changing minds or guided discovery?* Keynote address presented at the 1993 European Congress of Behaviour and Cognitive Therapies, London, United Kingdom.

Padesky, C. A. (1996). *Guided discovery using Socratic dialogue.* Newport Beach, CA: Center for Cognitive Therapy.

Parsons, T. D., & Rizzo, A. A. (2008). Affective outcomes of virtual reality exposure therapy for anxiety and specific phobias: A meta-analysis. *Journal of Behavior Therapy and Experimental Psychiatry, 39,* 250–261. doi:10.1016/j.jbtep.2007.07.007

Paul, R., & Elder, E. (2006). *The thinker's guide to the art of Socratic questioning.* Dillon Beach, CA: Foundation for Critical Thinking Press.

Powers, M. B., & Emmelkamp, P. M. G. (2008). Virtual reality exposure therapy for anxiety disorders: A meta-analysis. *Journal of Anxiety Disorders, 22,* 561–569. doi:10.1016/j.janxdis.2007.04.006

Powers, M. B., Halpern, J. M., Ferenschak, M. P., Gillihan, S. J., & Foa, E. B. (2010). A meta-analytic review of prolonged exposure for posttraumatic stress disorder. *Clinical Psychology Review, 30,* 635–641. doi:10.1016/j.cpr.2010.04.007

Renshaw, K. D., Blais, R. K., & Caska, C. M. (2011). Distress in spouses of combat veterans with PTSD: The importance of interpersonally based cognitions and behaviors. In S. M. Wadsworth & D. Riggs (Eds.), *Risk and resilience in U.S. military families* (pp. 69–84). doi:10.1007/978-1-4419-7064-0_4

Resick, P. A., Galovski, T. E., Uhlmansiek, M. O., Scher, C. D., Clum, G. A., & Young-Xu, Y. (2008). A randomized clinical trial to dismantle components of cognitive processing therapy for posttraumatic stress disorder in female victims of interpersonal violence. *Journal of Consulting and Clinical Psychology, 76,* 243–258. doi:10.1037/0022-006X.76.2.243

Resick, P. A., Monson, C. M., & Chard, K. M. (2008). *Cognitive processing therapy: Veteran/military version.* Washington, DC: U.S. Department of Veterans Affairs.

Resick, P. A., Monson, C. M., & Gutner, C. (2007). Psychological treatments for PTSD. In M. J. Friedman, T. M. Keane, & P. A. Resick (Eds.), *Handbook of PTSD: Science and practice* (pp. 330–358). New York, NY: Guilford Press.

Resick, P. A., Nishith, P., & Griffin, M. G. (2003). How well does cognitive–behavioral therapy treat symptoms of complex PTSD? An examination of child sexual abuse survivors within a clinical trial. *CNS Spectrums, 8,* 340–355.

Resick, P. A., Nishith, P., Weaver, T. L., Astin, M. C., & Feuer, C. A. (2002). A comparison of cognitive processing therapy with prolonged exposure and a waiting condition for the treatment of chronic posttraumatic stress disorder in female rape victims. *Journal of Consulting and Clinical Psychology, 70,* 867–879. doi:10.1037/0022-006X.70.4.867

Resick, P. A., Williams, L. F., Suvak, M. K., Monson, C. M., & Gradus, J. L. (2012). Long-term outcomes of cognitive–behavioral treatments for posttraumatic stress disorder among female rape survivors. *Journal of Consulting and Clinical Psychology, 80,* 201–210. doi:10.1037/a0026602

Richards, D. A., Lovell, K., & Marks, I. M. (1994). Post-traumatic stress disorder: Evaluation of a behavioral treatment program. *Journal of Traumatic Stress, 7,* 669–680. doi:10.1002/jts.2490070412

Riggs, D. S., Rothbaum, B. O., & Foa, E. B. (1995). A prospective examination of symptoms of posttraumatic stress disorder in victims of nonsexual assault. *Journal of Interpersonal Violence, 10,* 201–214. doi:10.1177/0886260595010002005

Rosen, C. S., Chow, H. C., Finney, J. F., Greenbaum, M. A., Moos, R. H., Sheik, J. I., & Yesavage, J. A. (2004). VA practice patterns and the practice guidelines for treating posttraumatic stress disorder. *Journal of Traumatic Stress, 17,* 213–222. doi:10.1023/B:JOTS.0000029264.23878.53

Rosenheck, R., & Fontana, A. (1996). Race and outcome of treatment for veterans suffering from PTSD. *Journal of Traumatic Stress, 9,* 343–351. doi:10.1002/jts.2490090215

Rothbaum, B. O. (Ed.). (2006). *Pathological anxiety: Emotional processing in etiology and treatment.* New York, NY: Guilford Press.

Rothbaum, B. O., Foa, E. B., Riggs, D. S., Murdock, T., & Walsh, W. (1992). A prospective examination of post-traumatic stress disorder in rape victims. *Journal of Traumatic Stress, 5,* 455–475. doi:10.1002/jts.2490050309

Rutter, J. G., Friedberg, R. D., VandeCreek, L., & Jackson, T. L. (1999). *Innovations in clinical practice: A source book.* Sarasota, FL: Professional Resource Press.

Safran, J. D., & Segal, Z. V. (1990). *Interpersonal process in cognitive therapy.* New York, NY: Basic Books.

Sautter, F. J., Glynn, S. M., Thompson, K. E., Franklin, L., & Han, X. (2009). A couple-based approach to the reduction of PTSD avoidance symptoms: Preliminary findings. *Journal of Marital and Family Therapy, 35,* 343–349. doi:10.1111/j.1752-0606.2009.00125.x

Schmidt, N. B., Woolaway-Bickel, K., Trakowski, J., Santiago, H., Storey, J., Koselka, M., & Cook, J. (2000). Dismantling cognitive–behavioral treatment for panic disorder: Questioning the utility of breathing retraining. *Journal of Consulting and Clinical Psychology, 68,* 417–424. doi:10.1037//0022-006X.68.3.417

Schnurr, P. P., Lunney, C. A., & Sengupta, A. (2004). Risk factors for the development versus maintenance of posttraumatic stress disorder. *Journal of Traumatic Stress, 17,* 85–95. doi:10.1023/B:JOTS.0000022614.21794.f4

Schulz, P. M., Resick, P. A., Huber, L. C., & Griffin, M. G. (2006). The effectiveness of cognitive processing therapy for PTSD with refugees in a community setting. *Cognitive and Behavioral Practice, 13,* 322–331. doi:10.1016/j.cbpra.2006.04.011

Schumm, J. A., Fredman, S. J., Monson, C. M., & Chard, K. M. (2013). Cognitive–behavioral conjoint therapy for PTSD: Initial findings for Operations Enduring and Iraqi Freedom male combat veterans and their partners. *American Journal of Family Therapy, 41,* 277–287. doi:10.1080/01926187.2012.701592

Shnaider, P., Pukay-Martin, N. D., Fredman, S. J., Macdonald, A., & Monson, C. M. (in press). Effects of cognitive–behavioral conjoint therapy for PTSD on partners' psychological functioning. *Journal of Traumatic Stress.*

Surís, A., Link-Malcolm, J., Chard, K., Ahn, C., & North, C. (2013). A randomized clinical trial of cognitive processing therapy for veterans with PTSD related to military sexual trauma. *Journal of Traumatic Stress, 26,* 1–10. doi:10.1002/jts.21765

Surís, A., North, C., Adinoff, B., Powell, C. M., & Greene, R. (2010). Effects of exogenous glucocorticoid on combat-related PTSD symptoms. *Annals of Clinical Psychiatry, 22,* 274–279.

Taft, C. T., Watkins, L. E., Stafford, J., Street, A. E., & Monson, C. M. (2011). Posttraumatic stress disorder and intimate relationship problems: A meta-analysis. *Journal of Consulting and Clinical Psychology, 79,* 22–33. doi:10.1037/a0022196

Tarrier, N., Pilgrim, H., Sommerfield, C., Faragher, B., Reynolds, M., Graham, E., & Barrowclough, C. (1999). A randomized trial of cognitive therapy and imaginal exposure in the treatment of chronic posttraumatic stress disorder. *Journal of Consulting and Clinical Psychology, 67,* 13–18. doi:10.1037/0022-006X.67.1.13

Tarrier, N., Sommerfield, C., & Pilgrim, H. (1999). Relatives' expressed emotion (EE) and PTSD treatment outcome. *Psychological Medicine, 29*, 801–811. doi:10.1017/S0033291799008569

Tarrier, N., Sommerfield, C., Pilgrim, H., & Faragher, B. (2000). Factors associated with outcome of cognitive-behavioural treatment of chronic post-traumatic stress disorder. *Behaviour Research and Therapy, 38*, 191–202. doi:10.1016/S0005-7967(99)00030-3

Taylor, S., Thordarson, D. S., Maxfield, L., Fedoroff, I. C., Lovell, K., & Ogrodniczuk, J. (2003). Comparative efficacy, speed, and adverse effects of three PTSD treatments: Exposure therapy, EMDR, and relaxation training. *Journal of Consulting and Clinical Psychology, 71*, 330–338. doi:10.1037/0022-006X.71.2.330

Tchanturia, K., Anderluh, M. B., Morris, R. G., Rabe-Hesketh, S., Collier, D. A., Sanchez, P., & Treasure, J. L. (2004). Cognitive flexibility in anorexia nervosa and bulimia nervosa. *Journal of the International Neuropsychological Society, 10*, 513–520. doi:10.1017/S1355617704104086

Thase, M. E., & Beck, A. T. (1993). An overview of cognitive therapy. In J. H. Wright (Ed.), *Cognitive therapy with inpatients: Developing a cognitive milieu* (pp. 3–34). New York, NY: Guilford Press.

Tuerk, P. W., Yoder, M., Ruggiero, K. J., Gros, D. F., & Acierno, R. (2010). A pilot study of prolonged exposure therapy for posttraumatic stress disorder delivered via telehealth technology. *Journal of Traumatic Stress, 23*, 116–123. doi:10.1002/jts.20494

Turner, A. P., & Jakupcak, M. (2010). Behavioral activation for treatment of PTSD and depression in an Iraqi combat veteran with multiple physical injuries. *Behavioural and Cognitive Psychotherapy, 38*, 355–361. doi:10.1017/S1352465810000081

van Minnen, A., Harned, M. S., Zoellner, L., & Mills, K. (2012). Examining potential contraindications for prolonged exposure therapy for PTSD. *European Journal of Psychotraumatology, 3*, Article 18805. doi:10.3402/ejpt.v3i0.18805

Vaughan, K., Armstrong, M. S., Gold, R., O'Connor, N., Jenneke, W., & Tarrier, N. (1994). A trial of eye movement desensitization compared to image habituation training and applied muscle relaxation in post-traumatic stress disorder. *Journal of Behavior Therapy and Experimental Psychiatry, 25*, 283–291. doi:10.1016/0005-7916(94)90036-1

Wagner, A. W., Zatzick, D. F., Ghesquiere, A., & Jurkovich, G. J. (2007). Behavioral activation as an early intervention for posttraumatic stress disorder and depression among physically injured trauma survivors. *Cognitive and Behavioral Practice, 14*, 341–349. doi:10.1016/j.cbpra.2006.05.002

Wenzlaff, R. M., & Wegner, D. M. (2000). Thought suppression. *Annual Review of Psychology, 51*, 59–91. doi:10.1146/annurev.psych.51.1.59

Whisman, M. A. (1999). Marital dissatisfaction and psychiatric disorders: Results from the National Comorbidity Survey. *Journal of Abnormal Psychology, 108*, 701–706. doi:10.1037/0021-843X.108.4.701

Wolpe, J. (1969). *The practice of behavior therapy*. Oxford, United Kingdom: Pergamon Press.

Wright, J. H., Basco, M. R., & Thase, M. E. (2006). *Learning cognitive-behavior therapy: An illustrated guide*. Washington, DC: American Psychiatric Publishing.

Yehuda, R., Bierer, L., Pratchett, L., & Malowney, M. (2010). Glucocorticoid augmentation of prolonged exposure therapy: Rationale and case report. *European Journal of Psychotraumatology, 1*(10), Article 27. doi:10.3402/ejpt.v1i0.5643

Zayfert, C., & Becker, C. B. (2007). *Cognitive–behavioral therapy for PTSD: A case formulation approach*. New York, NY: Guilford Press.

Index

About the Authors

Candice M. Monson, PhD, is a professor of psychology and director of clinical training at Ryerson University in Toronto, Ontario. She is also an Affiliate of the Women's Health Sciences Division of the U.S. Veterans Affairs National Center for Posttraumatic Stress Disorder, where she previously served as deputy director. Dr. Monson is one of the foremost experts on traumatic stress and the use of individual and conjoint therapies to treat posttraumatic stress disorder (PTSD). She has published extensively on the development, evaluation, and dissemination of PTSD treatments more generally, as well as gender differences in violence perpetration and victimization.

Dr. Monson has been funded by the U.S. Department of Veterans Affairs, National Institute of Mental Health, Centers for Disease Control and Prevention, Department of Defense, and Canadian Institutes of Health Research for her research on interpersonal factors in traumatization and couple-based interventions for PTSD. She is a Fellow of the Canadian Psychological Association. She coauthored *Cognitive Processing Therapy: Veteran/Military Version* and is the original developer of cognitive-behavioral conjoint therapy for PTSD. Dr. Monson is well-known for her efforts in training clinicians in evidence-based interventions for PTSD.

Philippe Shnaider, MA, is a graduate student in the department of psychology at Ryerson University. His research focuses on examining the associations between PTSD, intimate relationships, and partners' psychological functioning, as well as how these factors change in individual- and couple-based interventions. Additionally, his research examines the associations between impairments in specific domains of psychosocial functioning and PTSD symptom clusters, with a focus on how changes in these variables occur with treatment. His clinical interests include the treatment of PTSD and anxiety disorders, as well as the use of couple-based interventions to treat individual mental health conditions. He is also involved in efforts to disseminate empirically based treatments for PTSD among front-line clinicians.